W0010289

"In the grand tradition of Marjorie Holmes's bestselling, *I've Got to Talk to Somebody, God*, author Anita Corrine Donihue writes straight from the heart and shares her conversations with God in a warm, easy style. She touches on every aspect of daily life: joy; sorrow; concern for family, friends, and strangers; confronting obstacles and overcoming self-doubt. The message is clear. The only way to successful living is to trust God and listen for His counsel in and for everything."

- Colleen L. Reece, *150 Books You Can Trust*,
six million copies sold

"Anita Donihue's daily prayers are Spirit-directed and serve as a useful model for those who desire to become more intimate with God. Anita's prayers, uniquely blended with scripture, woo us to the throne of grace."

- Nancy Nelson, Development Director, Warm Beach
Christian Camps and Conference Center

"Anita Donihue has the ability to pour out her heart to God in a very open and honest way in *Power Prayers Devotional*. Through her heart-felt prayers and selected scripture verses we are able to allow our own hearts to cry out to God in the same deep way."

-Martha Hadley, Nationally Syndicated Christian Radio
Personality for *The Martha Hadley Show*, and former host of
the Focus On the Family/CRISTA Ministries program,
Sharing Life Together with Martha Hadley

Power Prayers
Devotional

Power Prayers
Devotional

*180 Inspiring Meditations to Deepen Your
Relationship with the Heavenly Father*

ANITA CORRINE DONIHUE

BARBOUR BOOKS
An Imprint of Barbour Publishing, Inc.

Published by Barbour Books, an imprint of Barbour Publishing, Inc., P.O. Box 719, Uhrichsville, Ohio 44683, www.barbourbooks.com

Our mission is to publish and distribute inspirational products offering exceptional value and biblical encouragement to the masses.

Printed in China

To my readers:

May God richly bless you through these devotions.
May you truly experience His amazing power of prayer.

In Search of You

*H*ere I am, Lord. As I begin this new year, I look back to another beginning: one when I accepted You as my Savior. Oh, how I love being with You.

Once, I wasn't sure if You knew me. I seldom talked with You. I'm thankful for my friend who invited me to ask You to be my Savior. Although I didn't understand how it could be possible, I felt a longing in my heart to receive You.

I feared such a big decision. I wanted to control my life. I preferred everything mapped out, certain. I wondered how I could trust You to direct me when I didn't even know You. I wasn't sure about turning my entire existence over to Someone I hadn't seen.

I didn't do well with the way I lived before receiving You, Lord. Should I have died then, I wonder what my eternity would have been. I questioned why You wanted to be my Savior, and if You would care about me, through good or bad. I feared You might desert me, especially when I messed up.

Thank You for leading me to find You, dear Lord. Or did You find me? I'm so glad You revealed what it meant to receive You as my Savior. In Jesus' name, amen.

"I am the way, the truth, and the life.
No one comes to the Father except through Me."

JOHN 14:6 NKJV

Getting to Know about You

I'm grateful for how You kept urging me to get to know You, Lord. Once, my whirlwind life tossed me about like a rag doll. No matter how hard I tried, I couldn't solve my dilemmas. Things were just too difficult to untangle. I longed for joy and peace, but I could find none. Even though I hadn't yet received You as my Savior, You still showed me Your unfailing love and mercy. That's when I wanted to know more about You. Thank You for caring for me and really hearing my prayers.

Still, I wondered if there was more to praying than repeating the same words over and over—more than asking You for help out of my problems. When I sought You, Lord, You guided me to Your Bible. I'm still overwhelmed by the way Your Holy Spirit whispered, *"Come unto Me. Receive Me as your Lord and Savior."*

Thank You for tugging on my heartstrings, so I knew You were near. Through Your Son Jesus, You were only a prayer away. It was like the air I breathed. I couldn't see You, but I began to perceive You were real.

Thank You for never giving up on me, Lord. How appreciative I am for the way You showed me how to know more about You.

Therefore he is able to save completely
those who come to God through him,
because he always lives to intercede for them.
Hebrews 7:25 niv

Why Did I Treat You So?

While sipping a cup of tea in a restaurant today, Lord, I happened to notice a couple having lunch with their teenage boy and girl. Sadly, the teenagers showed impudent and argumentative attitudes toward their parents and each other. No matter how the parents tried to relate and make a pleasant lunch, the teens responded rudely.

I reflected back to the know-it-all behavior I sometimes displayed toward my parents during my teenage years and hung my head. How sorry I am for the grief I caused them. Why did I hurt them so? Forgive me, Lord.

I recalled the flippant attitude I also once had toward You before I became a Christian. No matter how much You tried to relate to me and guide me in the right way, I rebelled. Whenever I heard You whisper to my heart, I refused to listen. When You showered Your love upon me, I shrugged it off. I wanted everything my way.

Why did I treat You so? I caused grief for You, myself, and those around me. I'm sorry for my flippant, thoughtless ways, Lord. Thank You for not giving up on me. Thank You for forgiving and loving me.

For you were continually straying like sheep,
but now you have returned to the Shepherd
and Guardian of your souls.

1 PETER 2:25 NASB

11

Yielding to You

*B*efore I yielded to You, I was incredibly stubborn, Lord. At church, the pastor explained how to accept You as my Savior. He invited people to pray at Your altar. It seemed the pastor could peer into my soul and was talking directly to me.

I held off coming to You too long. When we all stood and prayed, my hands gripped the pew in front of me until my knuckles turned white. Still, You kept calling me.

Everywhere, all the time, I heard You talk to my heart. You patiently waited, while I turned my life into more confusion and disaster. I could sense You reaching out Your hand to me. Finally, I gave up and grabbed hold.

That night by my bedside where I knelt and prayed, I wholeheartedly gave You my life. There, You led me to Your throne of grace. What a new and amazing experience it was. Although I had prayed to You before, I was finally meeting You personally as my Savior. You, who are Master of everything, came into my heart.

A huge burden lifted from my shoulders when I gave You my wasted, sin-controlled life. An indescribable joy filled me. I could hardly wait to tell all my friends and family what You did for me.

*So from now on we regard no one
from a worldly point of view.
Though we once regarded Christ
in this way, we do so no longer.*
2 CORINTHIANS 5:16 NIV

Simplicity of Surrender

*O*nce I chose to ask You into my heart, it became simple to surrender to You. Somehow, You managed to melt my willful ways and help me open my eyes to Your unwavering love for me. When I gave up my will to You, the things that once tugged me away from You faded to total insignificance. I didn't feel I lost anything. Instead, I became aware that I gained everything. For the first time, I realized You truly cared about me. You knew how I felt. You kept my wants and dreams in mind. Most of all, You recognized what was, and what was not, best for my life.

How sweet Your ways became to me. Everything in my life, good and bad, I freely gave to You. I felt sorry to be laying the mess I had made of my life before You. I was amazed that You picked up my fragmented pieces without hesitation. Immediately, You took me into Your loving presence just the way I was. You were able to reach into my soul and write Your name upon my open, pliable heart at last.

Thank You, Lord, for gently tugging at my stubborn heartstrings and for helping me experience a simplicity of surrender to You—my Lord, my Hope, my all.

"For whoever desires to save his life will lose it, but whoever loses his life for My sake will find it. For what profit is it to a man if he gains the whole world, and loses his own soul?"

MATTHEW 16:25–26 NKJV

Repenting Prayer

*F*ather, I had no idea how it could be possible to be "born again." Through reading Your Bible and hearing my Christian friend explain that I had been physically born as a baby, I learned I could be born again spiritually into the family of God. I slowly started to understand and opened my heart's door, just a crack.

I knew I had sin in my life just like everyone else in this world. The only way I could come to You was through Your Son, Jesus. I wondered what I would need to do so I could receive Jesus as my Savior.

Thank You for the way my friend taught me to pray a repenting prayer. I was already sorry for my sins. All I had to do was tell You so and ask You to forgive me. In a flash, You did forgive me. Then I asked Jesus to become my Savior and for Your Holy Spirit to come into my life.

It was amazing how You made me Your born-again child. I had become a brand-new baby Christian. What a thrill it was to know You as my heavenly Father, Your Son as my Savior, and experience Your Holy Spirit in my life. Thank You, Father, for helping me to pray a repenting prayer and ask You into my heart.

*Peter said. . ."Repent, and let every one of you be baptized
in the name of Jesus Christ for the remission of sins;
and you shall receive the gift of the Holy Spirit."*

ACTS 2:38 NKJV

I Wish I Could See You

There was a time, Lord, when I felt seeing was the only way to believe. Although I couldn't see You, I'm glad I took that fearful step and accepted You as my Savior. Once I did, my whole world began to change. No longer did I go aimlessly through life. You gave me a purpose. You gave me love; I received that love and gave it back to You. You gave me a drive to share with anyone who listens all about what You did and are still doing for me.

When night falls, I know Your sun will return the next day. The moon also revisits at evening. When clouds hover overhead and the sun cannot be seen, I know it is there. Though unseen, I know You are here, too.

But I wish I could *see* You, Lord. I wish I could slip my fingers into Your nail-scarred hands. I long to gaze into Your eyes or touch the hem of Your robe. Once, I felt this way because I wanted to be sure You were real. Now I *know* Your loving presence dwells within me. But I still wish I could get just one glimpse of Your face.

Now, Lord, I will follow You by faith, not by sight. The more I walk and talk with You, the more I know You. Although I have never seen You, I thank You for being my Savior. Thank You for helping me to walk by faith and not by sight.

"No one has seen the Father except the one who is from God;
only he has seen the Father. Very truly I tell you,
the one who believes has eternal life."

JOHN 6:46–47 NIV

15

Another Chance

*W*hy did You have the patience to keep calling me? No matter how far I ran, You gave me another chance—and another—to receive You. Am I important to You?

My dear child, I love you with an everlasting love. You are dearer to Me than you can imagine. I am the Good Shepherd. You are My sheep. When you were lost, I followed you like a sheep gone astray. I didn't give up until you were safely in My fold.

Do You really know me?

I understand you better than anyone. I see when you sit and rise. I perceive your joys, your concerns, and everything you think. I knew you before you were formed in your mother's womb. I am even aware of how many hairs are on your head.

Will You always be with me?

No matter how high you ascend into the sky, no matter how deep you descend into the seas, I am here. And I shall lead you.

Will You love me through good and bad times?

Nothing can separate you from My love. Not tribulations, persecution, or famine—none of these can keep My love from you. Death or life or evil cannot. The angels will not. Be certain you are My child, whom I love and adore.

Thank You for another chance, Lord.

But the loving-kindness of the Lord is from everlasting to everlasting to those who reverence him.

PSALM 103:17–18 TLB

All Things Became New

*B*efore everything became new through You, Lord, I felt ashamed to tell people I loved You. I gave only a trite answer: "Yes, I'm a Christian." That was because I hadn't fully given You my heart, my all. After that night, the old things in my life were gone. Everything became new. No longer was I alone. From then on, Your presence filled me every day. It wasn't a big dramatic experience. I just knew You were there, loving and helping me.

Because Your Holy Spirit dwelled within me, my likes and dislikes changed. My life became Your temple. My heart, Your dwelling place. I lost interest in what I used to do that didn't please You. I still cared about my old friends. But I found a greater satisfaction in drawing closer to my newfound Christian acquaintances. They were always good about encouraging me in my walk with You. Best of all, You had become my Savior, my dearest Friend.

Thank You for never leaving me. Thank You for loving me through the good and bad times. Before I gave You my life, I was lost. Now I praise You, dear Lord, for I am found. Once I was spiritually blind, but now I see. I look forward to being Your child for the rest of my life.

Therefore, if anyone is in Christ,
thr new creation has come:
the old has gone, the new is here!
2 Corinthians 5:17 niv

How Can You Forgive Me?

*F*ather, I want to say how sorry I am for the things I did wrong before I started following You. I wasted so many years. How can You ever forgive me?

Is there anything I can do to make it up? Will years of good deeds pay my debt? No matter how much I try to do right, I can never repay You.

I already forgave you, My dear one. You don't need to make everything up. Your sin is gone forever. All I want is your love.

Are You happy with me, Lord? I'm really trying. Let me feel Your presence.

I am here. I never left you. You are the apple of My eye. As you love and obey Me, you continually make My heart glad. Come to Me. Listen to Me. Hear My words so You may live a life of joy unspeakable. You are My child, and I am your God.

Thank You again for forgiving me. Thank You for loving me, for being my heavenly Father. When I feel overwhelmed with regrets, let me remember Your forgiveness.

I said, "LORD, be merciful to me;
heal my soul, for I have sinned against You."
PSALM 41:4 NKJV

18

How Can I Forgive Myself?

*A*lthough You've forgiven me, Lord, regrets of my wasted years still haunt me. I can pardon others, but I'm having trouble forgiving myself. Help me, please. There's no way I can change my past. I've asked others for their mercy. I've even tried making things right. Teach me, now, to let things go.

The Bible says the two greatest commandments are to love the Lord with all your heart, soul, and mind; and love your neighbor as you do yourself. Does that mean loving myself is part of Your commandments? I think it does.

As You forgive me, I will endeavor to forgive myself. In so doing, I open my life to Your emotional and spiritual healing. No longer will I allow myself to be burdened by former things. Instead, I will trust You to make my life new.

When I make wrong choices, I'm grateful for how You pull me back to the right way. Thank You for Your constant love and guidance during these times.

Thank You, Father, for granting me the ability and compassion to forgive myself. If the remorse returns, I know it isn't of You. I will focus on Your love instead and enjoy Your grace and mercy.

Jesus said to him,
" 'You shall love the LORD your God with all your heart,
with all your soul, and with all your mind.'
This is the first and great commandment.
And the second is like it: 'You shall love your neighbor as yourself.' "
MATTHEW 22:37–39 NKJV

You Gave Me Faith

*B*efore I received You as my Savior, I didn't have faith that You could save me and make me Your child. I don't know why I doubted, Lord. Perhaps I simply couldn't comprehend Your love. Each time I was close to accepting You, I held back, unsure of Your desire to come into my heart.

Thank You for my friend who explained the way of salvation to me. Thank You for her letting me know faith wasn't something I could conjure up for myself. It could come only from You. She told me faith was like a grain of mustard seed—so tiny but one that can grow into a plant four to six feet tall. What I needed to do was exercise enough faith to invite You in. Now I realize You were waiting for me all along.

When I did this, the floodgates of Your blessings opened. In no time, my minuscule mustard seed–sized faith blossomed and grew beyond measure! Thank You, Lord, for the way I heard about Your wonderful love for me; for showing me in Your Bible how You died for my sins to save me; and for talking to my heart. Without a doubt, I am saved by grace through You—Jesus Christ, my Lord. I praise Your name! For now I belong to You.

So then faith comes by hearing,
and hearing by the word of God.
Romans 10:17 nkjv

Mercy Received and Given

I will bless You, O Lord, for Your mercy. I will remember all You do. Praise You for Your forgiveness. Thank You for healing my body, mind, and soul.

I'm grateful for the way You shower me with Your kindness. When I am weary, You strengthen me. When I am oppressed, You console me.

I'm continually humbled by how merciful and gracious You are. When I struggle and try to do things right, You are patient and understanding. How amazing is the way I can come to You and enjoy Your presence. How marvelous is Your mercy. You have removed my sins and cast them as far as the east is from the west. You love me like an upright parent cherishes a little child.

Your kindness is everlasting. Your truth shall endure throughout my future generations. Because I follow You, I look forward to You keeping Your righteous hand upon my children's children. How I thank You for doing this, for I have dedicated them to You. In the same way I receive mercy from You, let me give compassion to others. Teach me to be quick to forgive, to look beyond the faults and see each need.

Thank You for Your mercy and for teaching me to be merciful.

But from everlasting to everlasting
the Lord's love is with those who fear him,
and his righteousness with their children's children—
with those who keep his covenant
and remember to obey his precepts.
PSALM 103:17–18 NIV

You Are the Strength of My Life

When my friend asked You into his heart, I think Your angels burst into chorus. Thank You for giving him a new birthday, a spiritual one in accepting You. Thank You for giving me new life, as well. Doing good doesn't gain Your favor. It's simply loving You, because You forgave our sins and showed us a better way.

Once, my life was soiled and distorted. Now I am made clean, without a spot or wrinkle. I love You so much, Lord. How can any of us remain pure in Your eyes?

My little child, always remember I am the Way. I will give you the strength you need each day. Keep reading My Word and heeding its lessons. They will guide you along the right path. Think about them. Store them in your mind and heart so you won't sin against Me. Each time you seek Me you shall find Me. Abide in Me, and I shall abide in you.

Because I delight in You, O Lord, I will follow Your teachings. I will trust in Your promises day and night. They are more valuable to me than silver and gold. In all my ways I will acknowledge You. Thank You for being my Savior, for renewing my faith and staying power each day. Thank You for being with my friend, too.

*The LORD is my light and my salvation—
whom shall I fear? The LORD is the stronghold
of my life—of whom shall I be afraid?*
PSALM 27:1 NIV

Thank You for My Baptism

*F*ather, what an awesome experience it must have been for
those who witnessed Your Son, Jesus, being baptized. When
I first read about it, I felt as though I were there. I wondered why
someone so holy needed to be baptized. Jesus never had to repent
of any personal sins. Still, He set the example for me.

I wish I could have seen the Savior rise from the water and
witnessed Your Holy Spirit descend like a dove and settle on Him. I
wish I could have heard Your words thunder, *"This is My beloved Son,
in whom I am well pleased."*

After learning this, I realized I must be baptized. I wanted to
tell my friends and loved ones my sinful life had died—how You
washed my heart clean and flung my wrongs into the deepest sea.

I'll never forget my first step into the baptistery water, Father.
I glanced at the congregation and saw those who had faithfully
taught me of Your love. When asked if I loved You, I gave an
enthusiastic yes. Then into the water and up I came. I felt Your
dovelike holy presence settle upon me. From that time on, I have
never been the same.

Thank You for the example of Jesus and for the privilege of
following Him.

*As soon as Jesus was baptized, he went up out of the water. . . .
And a voice from heaven said, "This is my Son,
whom I love; with him I am well pleased."*
MATTHEW 3:16–17 NIV

23

I Will Serve You

*L*ord Jesus, I know You grieved as You saw my life heading for sin and destruction. How oblivious I was of Your offer to make me Your child. Then You began speaking to me over and over to turn from my wrongdoing and choose life, abundant and free. Once I heard the way of salvation, I had to make a choice. Would I serve and obey You or become a slave to sin?

I looked around me at the glorious things You created—the earth and sky, the sun and moon, the mountains, trees, and valleys. How could such things accidentally have fallen into place and synchronized so perfectly?

How heavily it weighed upon my heart when You made known that the wages of sin are eternal death. But Your free gift is eternal life through You, my Lord Jesus Christ. All I needed to do was trust You, God's Son, to save me and make me one of Your own.

Now I realize no one can serve two masters. I must either love or hate You. Or I must love or hate the devil. I choose You, Lord! It is You I shall follow and serve all the days of my life.

[God said,] "Choose life, that both you and your descendants may live;
that you may love the LORD your God, that you may obey His voice,
and that you may cling to Him, for He is your life
and the length of your days."

DEUTERONOMY 30:19–20 NKJV

Everyday Friend

*T*hank You, dear Father, for being my Friend every hour of every day. I praise You for Your constant presence, for the way You walk with me and talk to my heart.

When I get so involved that I'm not aware of Your presence, thank You for still being near. Loving. Helping. Protecting. Guiding.

I love You so much, more than I can even express. How grateful I am for Your becoming my heavenly Father and being with me all the time, in any circumstances.

My little child, I am always here with you. My love and friendship are unconditional and never failing. I love you with an everlasting love. In good times, I rejoice with you. In your trials, I hurt for you and comfort you as a little one is consoled by his mother.

When you are hungry, I feed you. When you are thirsty, I give you a drink from My vast well of living water. When you are frightened and confused, I am here to encourage and lead you. I will never abandon or forsake you during your storms of life. Each time you call on Me, I am here, in your heart. I am your Friend, now and forever.

" 'Fear not, for I am with you;
be not dismayed, for I am your God.
I will strengthen you, yes, I will help you,
I will uphold you with My righteous right hand.' "
Isaiah 41:10 NKJV

25

Your Family

Thank You for adopting me into Your family, Father. Along with my earthly lineage, You have made me a part of the heritage of God.

Like several of my friends who have chosen to adopt and love their children, I realize You also have done this with me. Now I have a relationship with You—and am related to You as well. This is beyond my scope. How glorious. How awesome!

What a blessing it is to be somewhere and recognize another who loves You, because of Your Spirit's reflection in his or her life. When this happens, it never ceases to fill me with awe. Brothers and sisters in the Lord, they say. What a marvelous inheritance I've gained in my new family of God. Thank You for the many ways we learn to care. May we always treat one another kindly, with patience and love.

Just like with my family from birth, there may be times of disappointment and hurt. When these times come, I pray for direction, forgiveness, and healing. Even though I'm a part of Your family, I know we still struggle with shortcomings. Help me to still reflect Your pure, unwavering love.

Thank You for being the head of my Christian family and being the source of my comfort and strength.

But to all who received him, he gave the right to become
children of God. All they needed to do
was to trust him to save them.
JOHN 1:11–12 TLB

A Brand-New Life

I am continually filled with wonder when I think of my brand-new life with You, Lord. In receiving You, I have been able to experience all You give me. How I praise You for this.

Now You call me by name. You have made me Your own. Each time I pass through difficult waters, I know I will not be swept away; for You are with me, holding my hand. When I go through fiery trials, You walk before me as my Shield and Defender.

You are my Lord, my God—the Holy One who rules over all. You created me in Your image. You made me for Your glory. To You I give honor and adoration and praise. To You I give the whole of my life.

I'm grateful for the way You show me how to put the past behind and press forward into the new life You now provide. I wonder what lies ahead. I look forward with great anticipation as we walk life's road together.

Because you are my Lord, I will trust everything to You. Help me remember to depend not only on my own understanding. I will acknowledge You and follow as You direct my paths.

"Do not remember the former things, nor consider the things of old. Behold, I will do a new thing, now it shall spring forth; shall you not know it? I will even make a road in the wilderness and rivers in the desert."

ISAIAH 43:18–19 NKJV

Thank You for Receiving Me

I thank You, Lord Jesus, that along with my receiving You as my Savior, You took me into Your arms and received me as Your own. I know You loved me before I was ever born.

I can't comprehend how You prayed for me in the Garden of Gethsemane, knowing full well You were about to die for my sins.

I read in my Bible that before You died, no one could come directly to Your Father except chosen priests. In the temple, there was a Holy of Holies, with a huge, thick curtain keeping those who loved the heavenly Father from coming directly into His presence. It was because they weren't free from sin. When You died on the cross, that huge, thick curtain (or veil) mysteriously split from top to bottom!

Those who accepted You as their Savior were no longer separated from the holy presence of the Father. For You sacrificed Yourself on the cross and washed away with Your blood the sins of those who accepted You.

Because You died for me and I asked You into my heart, I can come to You anytime, anywhere, and be welcomed into Your presence. Thank You, Lord, for receiving me as Your child.

Therefore, since we have a great high priest who has ascended into heaven,
Jesus the Son of God, let us hold firmly to the faith we profess. . . .
Let us then approach God's throne of grace with confidence.
HEBREWS 4:14, 16 NIV

Who Can Compare to You?

*H*ow wonderful You are, my God. How awesome it is to come into Your presence. I worship You with joyfulness and thanksgiving, for I know You are my Lord, my God. You are the Creator of everything. You wrapped Your fingers around the mountains and formed their highest points. You reached down and dipped Your hand into the depths of the earth. You scooped out huge cavities and filled them with oceans, lakes, and rivers. You skillfully shaped the dry ground.

You took the care to plan my distinct being, before I was even formed in my mother's womb. With a puff of breath and a thump to my chest, You set my heart and lungs into motion. You made me the person I am. Thank You for allowing me to be Your child and for being my heavenly Father.

Who can compare to You, my God? There is no other so great. You are all-knowing, forever loving. Your mercy to me shall endure forever, even beyond my earthly life! Your indisputable love shall last throughout future generations. Forever, You shall be exalted among the nations. Forever, You shall be exalted over the earth!

I come to You and bow down, for You are my Lord, my Maker. You, Lord, are the true God. There is no other who can compare to You.

Who is like you, Lord God Almighty,
You, Lord, are mighty
and your faithfulness surrounds you.
Psalm 89:8 niv

You Surpass All Else

*W*hom can I call, my Lord, besides You? You surpass everyone, everything in heaven, and all the galaxies, my God. You matter most, for You are my strength and my portion. You are my source of food and drink. You are my Lord and Savior forever! When I despair, You lift me up. You are my greatest joy. How lovingly You watch over me as Your own. In You rests my spiritual inheritance. In You I place my every hope.

O holy God, You exceed all else. How immense and powerful and awe-inspiring You are! Before You, there was no other. No one shall come after You; for You, Lord, are the Beginning and the End. You and You alone are Lord over all. Aside from You, I have no origin.

Before the ancient days, You were there. Before heaven and earth, You were, You are, and You ever shall be. When You speak, Your will comes to pass. No one else can reverse it; for You are Creator and Ruler over everything. Your mouth declares all truthfulness. Your never-ending words cannot be rescinded.

Before You every knee shall bow, and every tongue shall confess, " 'In the LORD alone are deliverance and strength' " (Isaiah 45:24 NIV). You alone, O God, surpass all else!

Because Your lovingkindness is better than life,
my lips shall praise You. Thus I will bless You.
PSALM 63:3–4 NKJV

I Belong to You

$\mathcal{T}$hank You, Father, for allowing me to belong to You. I praise You for adopting me as Your own. Since I accepted Your Son, Jesus, as my Savior, I am no longer separated from Your holy family. I desire to honor You all the days of my life and cling to You as a branch does to the vine. You are my Vine, and I am one of Your branches. It is only in being grafted to You that I'm able to accomplish anything of eternal value. I can do whatever You ask of me through You, Jesus Christ, my Lord.

Because You took me in as Your own, I will praise You from my inmost being. With all my heart, I give honor to You. Thank You for loving me as the apple of Your eye—for hiding me in Your strong arms and protecting me from wrong. I will never forget Your many blessings.

Thank You for Your forgiveness. When I come to You, You pump life into me the same way subsistence goes from the vine to the branches. I praise You for making Your ways known and showering me with Your compassion and graciousness. I am Your child and You are my heavenly Father. With every fiber of my being, I give honor to You.

Keep me as the apple of Your eye;
hide me under the shadow of Your wings.

Psalm 17:8 NKJV

Let My Thoughts Honor You

When the temptations and confusion of this world press around me, Lord, let my thoughts be focused on what pleases You. May my mind meditate on Your teachings throughout my day and night. Let me drink in Your priceless words of scripture. Hide them in my memory bank, I pray, so I may apply them to my daily life. Grant me strength and guidance through Your Holy Spirit, to honor You in what I watch, read, and observe. May all of this be delightful and pleasing to You.

When the dry winds of stress flurry around me, I will not be consumed, for my spiritual roots sink deeply in You. With Your help, my leaves shall not wither. They shall produce the priceless fruits of Your Spirit: unselfish love, joyfulness, harmony, patience, kindness, goodness, faithfulness, sensitivity, and self-control.

I will think on all Your marvelous works and reflect on the mighty things You do, for Your ways, O God, are holy. I marvel at how You display Your astounding power. I treasure the recollections of the many instances You have placed Your blessings upon me.

Let me meditate on You every day. Guide my decisions. May each one bring respect to You. Guide my mind and heart, I pray. In all my ways I want to honor You with pure, obedient thoughts, words, and deeds.

But his delight is in the law of the LORD,
and in His law he meditates day and night.

PSALM 1:2 NKJV

My Heart Is Your Home

Oh, how I praise You, Lord, for entering my heart and making my soul Your dwelling place. It goes beyond my comprehension. I praise You for showering me with Your loving-kindness. You looked beyond my sins and saw my needs. When I bowed in repentance before You, You washed my heart clean and made me as pure as fresh snow.

Welcome to my heart, Your home, dear Lord. May it honor You in every way. Wherever I go, whatever I say or do, I know You are with me—fully aware of my every move. When I start to go the wrong way and You nudge me, give me strength to turn around and leave. My heart is Your home, Lord. May no person or thing be allowed through its door unless it is honorable to You.

Search the corners of my heart so it remains a holy place for You to dwell. Help me rid myself of unpleasant dust bunnies hidden from human eyes. Fill the corners with Your loving, holy presence. With my whole heart I seek You so I won't wander from Your way. I will treasure Your wise words and hold them within me so I will not sin against You. I pray for You to always grant me Your presence in my heart, Your home.

Create in me a new, clean heart, O God,
filled with clean thoughts and right desires.
Psalm 51:10 tlb

My Mind Turns to You in the Morn

*G*ood morning, Lord. Thank You for last night's rest and for providing me with a fresh start today. Thank You for hearing my prayers and acknowledging my deepest concerns. I love this time when all is quiet—when I hear You speak to my heart and pay heed to the whispers from my lips. How grateful I am to be able to lay my requests before You and wait in trusting expectation for Your will.

Thank You for allowing me to come into Your presence. I bow before You in reverence. Lead me in Your ways of righteousness. Throughout my day, I will take refuge in Your counsel and be glad, for Your wisdom is greater than any other. I shall keep You foremost in my thoughts and give You the sacrifice of my will. In all things, I exalt Your name.

With each task I seek to accomplish, each decision I must make, I will reflect and honor You, O Lord. You are my strength, my Shield, my Rock, and my Defender. I praise You for going before me—for being at my right hand and my left, before and behind me. Each time I face uncertainties, thank You for straightening my path.

Praise You, Lord, for being within my mind and heart.

O Lord, in the morning thou dost hear my voice;
in the morning I prepare a sacrifice for thee, and watch.
Psalm 5:3 rsv

My Lips Give You Honor

May my prayers give You honor, dear Lord. May what I say to others make You glad. Guard my tongue so gossip and cutting remarks are replaced with words that soothe and heal.

Help me speak the truth. Help me seek answers, instead of escapes from problems. I will have no part of cursing or tainted language. Instead, I look to You for words of innocence, purity, and caution—filled with life and health.

You are holy, Lord. You are the essence of life and all that is good. In You I find hope, a purpose to do right, and words filled with exultation. My heart is full of gratitude. I praise Your holy name. Your righteousness and saving grace are measureless. Wherever I go, I want to tell others how wonderful You are. Over and over You put a new song of praise in my mouth. Because of this, others hear and come to You. How awesome! How marvelous, the way Your Spirit works!

How delightful are the words from Your Bible. Whenever I speak them and pay homage to You, they are sweeter than honey to my lips. Accept my words of adoration, O Lord. Continue to teach me Your ways. Let all I say give honor to You.

My mouth is filled with your praise,
declaring your splendor all day long.
PSALM 71:8 NIV

Harmonizing Praise

*P*raise You, O Lord. I feel Your love stay within me. Like a beautiful melody coming full circle, our love and communication weave back and forth between us. Holy, holy, holy are You, Lord. I'm blessed to receive You and give You praise. How fulfilling to talk things over—You and I. You tune my heart. I strike a chord. You give me words. I lift them back to You in honor and gratitude—praise in perfect harmony.

You are my one true God. You created everything and worked it all together. You wrought heaven and earth. Perhaps the angels sang as You made it all. You caused everything to have life. You brought me into this world. You heard my first cry. Though no one else could understand my squall of protest, You did; for You know me inside out.

From the moment I burst into this world, You hummed a soothing lullaby only I could hear. All through my years, I have heard You strike the chords in my heart and give me reason to love and praise You. You, dear Lord, have taken good and bad times and mixed them skillfully together for good with Your loving hand. You, my Author and Composer, have written our harmonizing songs of praise.

We love Him because He first loved us.
1 JOHN 4:19 NKJV

I Give You Glory

*W*ith all my heart, I praise You. With every fiber of my being, I give You glory. Each morning, I thank You for being so good to me. Your loving-kindness is better than life itself.

Each evening, I rejoice in Your remaining near. I pray that every living thing will give You glory. May my body, mind, and soul be holy and glorify You. When I think of the many things You do for me, there is so little I can do in return. No matter what comes my way, I will praise and glorify You.

Worthy are You, O Lamb of God. Worthy are You to receive power and riches and wisdom and strength and honor and glory. Even the heavens declare Your glory. Your name is majestic throughout the galaxies and over all the earth. Young and elderly sing Your praises. Only You are glorious and mighty enough to triumph over wrong.

Who am I that You are mindful of me? Am I only a speck of dust in Your vast creation? What of my loved ones? Do You care about them? And their children and grandchildren? I know You care, for You died on the cross to save all who believe in You.

I give You glory and adulation and praise, Lord. Through all my days, I will honor You.

Sing to the Lord, all the earth! Sing of his glorious name!
Tell the world how wonderful he is.
How awe-inspiring are your deeds, O God!
How great your power!
PSALM 66:1–3 TLB

Let My Memories Honor You

Something happened today that triggered some terrible memories, Lord. Before I knew it, my mind flooded with anxiety, hurt, and bitterness. Then You brought words of comfort to mind. Although the time I recalled was terrible, You helped me commit to memory the incredible way You rescued victory from defeat.

In the midst of life's trials, let me honor You with the memories of Your love and compassion. I praise You that You are there for me in all circumstances. Let me bless You, O Lord, with my memories. May I always consider the marvelous benefits You have given me. Thank You for how You forgave my iniquities and saved me from a life of waste and self-destruction. Let me never forget the many times You have crowned me with Your tender mercies and loving compassion.

When things were tough financially, You provided for my needs. During times of illness, You helped me get well and renewed my strength. How grateful I am for the way You showed me kindness and patience when I made unwise decisions. Thank You for Your forgiveness and for helping me start over. How grateful I feel for the ways You have guided me through situations and made my faith stronger because of them. How blessed I am, Lord, for treasured memories provided by You.

I bless the holy name of God with all my heart.
Yes, I will bless the Lord and not forget the glorious things
he does for me. . . . He fills my life with good things!
Psalm 103:1–2, 5 TLB

I Honor You with My Love

I love You so much, Lord. Yet no matter how great my love, it can't compare to the love You give me. I want to honor You with my love. Show me how to care for others with the same unselfish kindness You give me. Fill me with Your Holy Spirit. Use me to give them Your love. As You direct my life, You generate my sensitivity.

You *are* love, O Lord. As I live in You, I learn to care more for others; for You live in me. I feel the warm compassion of Your Holy Spirit within me everywhere I go. I love You because You first loved me. I want to honor You by doing whatever You ask and not expect any recognition in return. Because You died for me, You have helped me give up my old selfish life I once had. Now it is centered on the things that honor and please You. Help me remember to care for others as much as You do for me. Grant me enough love to look beyond the faults and see the needs—in the same way You did mine. Instead of being selfish, I want to become generous. Instead of being bitter, I want to show compassion. I want to revere You, Lord, and love the same way You do.

So you see, our love for him comes
as a result of his loving us first.
1 JOHN 4:19 TLB

My Endeavors Honor You

I used to have lofty dreams and goals of my own desire. No matter how hard I tried, things didn't turn out right. That was before I met You and asked You to become Lord of my life.

When I gave everything to You, including my endeavors, my life changed. Now I desire what is pleasing to You. I dream the dreams and set the goals You and I talk about together. I don't want to go off on a tangent anymore. Now I set goals in compliance with Your will. You know me well, Lord; and You recognize what is best for me. I praise You for giving me a life filled with peace, joy, and fulfillment.

In all these things, I delight in You. To You I commit my ways. May my greatest endeavor be to love others as You love me. Each day I pray for You to help me make righteous choices so I can glorify You. I don't feel frustrated when others succeed, and I'm not leaping over giant buildings! You have a plan for me. No longer do I stew in anger over some who carry out wicked schemes. Instead, I stand and wait in eager anticipation of Your plans! With all my strength, through all my days, let my endeavors honor You.

Commit everything you do to the Lord.
Trust him to help you do it, and he will.
Your innocence will be clear to everyone.
He will vindicate you with the blazing light of
justice shining down as from the noonday sun.

Psalm 37:5–6 tlb

The Calling

*I*t started as a nudge, when I first felt You calling me. It was so subtle, I barely noticed. Still, You kept beckoning. You had a plan of what You wanted me to do for You.

You gradually placed things in my mind and gave me a dream. I wondered if (or how) it would fit into my future. Little did I realize that when You call someone, You have Your own ways and timing to make it happen. Long before I became aware of Your bidding, You were preparing me.

You soon gave me a burning desire to follow Your lead. It was constantly in my heart and mind. How could it come about? I trusted You and felt complete peace. There is no element of time with You, Lord, and no challenges are too difficult.

The day came when You showed me how to answer Your call. I wanted to follow, step-by-step. It was hard, Lord, but You helped and led me. Your mission for me still isn't easy, and I ask for Your help. You grant me the strength and wisdom I need. Perhaps I'll never know the miracles wrought in the lives of others because of Your calling to me. In all I say and do, may I give You honor and praise.

[Jesus said,] "Whoever serves me must follow me;
and where I am, my servant also will be.
My Father will honor the one who serves me."

John 12:26 niv

My Gift of Praise

*W*hat can I give You, Lord, that You haven't already imparted to me? All I have to offer are honor and praise. I come before You on my knees with adoration and thanksgiving. I praise You for the wonderful things You do for me. I am grateful for Your loving care.

I praise You for the words You teach me—for how they enrich my life and give me wisdom. Thank You for all the things on this earth You have provided for me to enjoy. Thank You for creating me and being my Father. I praise You for purchasing my soul with a great price and saving me through Your Son, Christ Jesus. I praise You for allowing me to represent You by being a Christian. I praise You for the presence of Your awesome, strengthening Holy Spirit.

Wherever I go, I will tell others of the glory of Your name and what You do in my life. Each day I will boast of Your constant, holy ways. Each day I will tell the discouraged to take heart because You love them, too. Through the good and the bad of life, I will continually speak of Your glory and grace, for *You* are my joy, my triumph, my security. In You, Father, I place my trust. In all things, I bring You honor and praise.

I will praise You, O LORD, with my whole heart;
I will tell of all Your marvelous works.
I will be glad and rejoice in You;
I will sing praise to Your name, O Most High.
PSALM 9:1–2 NKJV

42

A Holy Life

I long to live a holy life for You, Lord Jesus. Yet the more I've tried, the more I have failed. Like Paul, I desire to do what's right. But in a short time, I've often messed up. What I've done isn't the good I want to do. And the wrongs I don't want to do keep cropping up. I love Your ways, dear Lord, and want to be like You.

You overcame sin and temptation while You were here on earth. You are the Son of God. Still, Your human example helps me. You went off alone regularly to talk with Your Father. The Bible says You know Him well, and He knows You. Is this what gave You strength? While spending forty days in the desert fasting and praying to Your Father, You overcame temptation. Filled with the Holy Spirit, You conquered its lure with scripture. Now I understand, Lord. I realize being tempted isn't a sin. Help me fight temptation with scripture from my Bible. Fill me with Your Spirit, and remind me to run like crazy from all appearances of evil.

You know me, Lord, and I know You. When I mess up, thank You for Your forgiveness and for helping me start over. I will fix my thoughts on You and remember how to honor You with a holy life.

"Consecrate yourselves and be holy,
because I am the LORD your God.
Keep my decrees and follow them.
I am the LORD, who makes you holy."
LEVITICUS 20:7–8 NIV

You Are My Heavenly Father

*D*o You always understand how I feel, Father? Are You happy for me when I'm in high spirits? Do You really empathize with me when I'm sad? Do You know how I feel when frustration and anger in me reach a boiling point? Are You with me when I bolt up in bed at night from a bad dream? Surely You know and care; for each time I call on Your name, I experience peace. I sense Your pleasure when I share my joys with You. Whenever I cry for help, You calm me and give me peace.

My little child, I know you better than you do yourself. I have searched your heart and am aware of everything about you. My presence is with you when you fall asleep and when you awaken. I see when you come and go. I perceive the words you are about to say before you speak. I am familiar with all your ways.

I go before and behind you. I keep My hand upon your head and watch over you. No matter where you are, I am there, holding tightly onto you. I do this because I love you, and you belong to Me.

Thank You for being my heavenly Father. Thank You for knowing and loving me.

As a father has compassion on his children,
so the LORD has compassion on those who fear him;
for he knows how we are formed.

PSALM 103:13–14 NIV

Before I Was Born

*F*ather, when I was a child, I dreamed of being a parent someday. I wondered how many children I would have. What would they be like? Would I have boys or girls? I wanted to be the best parent ever. Did You know me before I was born? Was I a soul in heaven You loved and cared for? Did You plan for me to be brought here? At this place? This time?

I feel You once wrapped me securely in Your loving arms, long ago. Being with You in heaven seems familiar. Was this my first home?

Even before you were conceived in your mother's womb, I knew you and consecrated you as My own. You were no mistake. Before all time, I had a plan for you. I created your inmost being as I carefully knit you together. In the depths of that secret place, I took your tiny, unformed body and molded it into something wonderful. I formed your nose, your fingers and toes—even your strands of hair. I knew your every little crease and fold. You are My masterpiece, My unique and lovely soul. I loved you before time. I love you now and forever.

I am grateful, Father, for Your planning and wanting me. I'm so glad You made me.

*My frame was not hidden from you
when I was made in the secret place.*
PSALM 139:15 NIV

45

In Your Image

*W*hat a thrill we received when each of our children was born, Father. I still remember their first cries—unique, individual. I can almost feel their tiny fingers wrapped around mine and see their daddy's proud gaze. And how those babies looked! A special combination of my husband and me.

Was I created like You, Father? How can I be the image of You, my awesome God? How fearfully and wonderfully made I am!

I created both male and female in My image. You are a reflection of Me. You are My very own dear one. I have made you to be My offspring—My child. In Me, you live and move and are.

It was no accident, the time and place you were born. From the beginning, I set My special plan for you into motion. It is true things would not always go smoothly for you. But all through your life, I have and will be with you as your heavenly Father. Even though you are made in My image, I give you free will. Choose to remain close to Me and reflect My purity, My child. I want you to be filled with joy and for you to experience the calling I give you.

Thank You, Father. In You, I will live and move and exist!

"For in him we live and move and have our being. . . .
We are his offspring."
ACTS 17:28 NIV

You Know My Number of Hairs

I'm amazed how You number my hairs, Father. On days I'm frustrated and feel like pulling some out, I must keep You pretty busy! You know me on the outside, and You surely understand me through and through. You share my pain when I lack confidence. You weep with me when I mourn. You nudge me to show mercy to those who wrong me. You help me find peace amid stress. Thank You for meeting my needs—for teaching me to rejoice during times of trouble.

I praise You for peace of heart and mind. How awesome, the way You allow me to come into Your presence. How good You are to change my heart, Father. When I am unsure, You encourage me. When fiery trials come, You go before me. Instead of worrying, I will remember the flowers and the fields and how You even see when one sparrow falls. How grateful I am that I matter more to You than these, for I am Your child.

I want you to tell others these things I reveal to you in quiet, dear child. This way they, too, can get to know Me more.

How wonderful You are, Father, for knowing me so well.

[Jesus said,] "What is the price of five sparrows?
A couple of pennies? Not much more than that.
Yet God does not forget a single one of them.
And he knows the number of hairs on your head!
Never fear, you are far more valuable to him
than a whole flock of sparrows."
LUKE 12:6–7 TLB

No Higher Than the Ceiling?

Sometimes I feel my prayers go no higher than the ceiling. I get depressed, Father, and I don't sense Your presence. Do my pleas just bounce around the room and lifelessly crash to the floor, no matter how hard I pray? Can You hear me, Father? Why do You not answer? You say You love me, so why are You not with me?

I want to feel You near. You are my all-knowing God. You made me. Surely You understand my heart. I will continue to cry out to You and pray for Your closeness. No matter what, I will trust in You and not doubt. I will praise You with all my heart.

Here I am, My child. I have been with you all along. All you had to do was stop and listen.

Thank You, Father. I'm learning that when I give You my love and praise, I then recognize Your glorious presence. Help me open my heart to You more. Praising You breaks down barriers so I can draw closer to You.

Thank You for being near. I bring my requests to You. I know You will answer. I understand my time isn't always Your time. My thoughts aren't always Your all-knowing thoughts. I feel Your comfort and assurance. I rest in You, Father, for You are good to me.

*Come near to God
and he will come near to you.*
JAMES 4:8 NIV

Do You Think of Me Often?

*E*ven though our children are grown now, Father, they and their families are often on my mind. I enjoy each time we get together and talk. Still, as much as I love and want the best for them, You must care for them and me all the more.

Your Bible says I am in Your thoughts, and Your plans for me are better than I can imagine. It's difficult for me to comprehend why You love me so. Perhaps it is as a devoted Father is to His child. Day after day, I am filled with delight, and I rejoice in Your loving presence.

You are precious to Me, dear one. I watch over you all the time! The sum of My hopes for you is far greater than grains of sand. I have marvelous things I want to do for you. My plans will exceed your highest hopes. If I were to tell them to you all at once, you wouldn't be able to fathom them.

How great is My love I want to lavish on you, merely because I am your heavenly Father, and you are My child. Listen to Me and keep My ways. Remain close, and you shall have a life filled with peace and joy beyond measure.

My thoughts shall be Your thoughts, heavenly Father; my ways, Your ways.

How precious it is, Lord, to realize that you are thinking about me constantly! I can't even count how many times a day your thoughts turn towards me.
Psalm 139:17–18 TLB

Your Plans for Me

*W*alking with You is the most excellent journey I've ever taken, Father. The adventure is trusting You when I can't see around the next bend. More than anything, I want to stay within Your will. I want to be sure my plans are in line with Yours.

You are in charge. I search for Your will through prayer. I explore the lessons in Your Bible. Remind me to seek wise advice of Christians and focus on Your purpose, instead of notions of those who don't know You. You are my heavenly Father. You know what is best.

I belong to You and am confident in Your plans for me. You promise in Your Word that Your direction will help and never harm me. No matter life's circumstances, Father, Your ways shall stand firm and true.

I have so many wonders and blessings in store for you, My child, that you will not be able to count them—plans for the present and more for the future. Not only are they for you, but for your children, your children's children—even for those who have not yet been born! My hand is already on them, too. Seek Me, and I will tell you great and incredible things you have yet to know.

Thank You, Father. I will fit into Your plans, for You are my God.

"For I know the plans that I have for you,"
declares the LORD, "plans for welfare [well-being]
and not for calamity to give you a future and a hope."
JEREMIAH 29:11 NASB

Love Everlasting

*Y*ou're so compassionate in the way You give Your love. How thankful I am for Your being my eternal Father. Thank You for calling me Your child. You even know my name. Your love goes beyond limits. It's unconditional. It's never ending. When I'm at my best, I feel Your care.

When I feel down and complain, You are still near. Even when I make poor decisions, You help me through and set my feet on the right path. You are dear to me, Father. I love You so much. At Your feet I bow, awaiting Your direction. There's no other like You. Now and forever, You will be first in my life.

Before time, in the present, and forever, I, your heavenly Father, cherish you with an inexhaustible love. With tenderness, I draw you closely to Me. I do this, My dear one, so you may know My Son. Each time you demonstrate love, I am glad. From everlasting to everlasting is My love for you, because You revere Me and act upon My precepts. I will always shower My compassion upon you, for I am your Lord and Redeemer.

I will remember Your promise of choosing me from the beginning. Thank You for Your love and encouragement. I praise You, Father God. I love You with the love You first gave me.

The Lord had said. . .
I have loved you, O my people,
with an everlasting love;
with lovingkindness I have drawn you to me.
JEREMIAH 31:3 TLB

Perfect Father

$\mathcal{F}$ather, I always wanted to be a perfect parent. Our children are my loves, my pride, my hope for the future. No matter how I try, though, I can't do everything right. In spite of my errors, I'm grateful for the good in our children. Thank You for healing hurts and helping to make things right. Always keep us close, Father.

Thank You for my dad. How dear he is to me. Thank You for the way we love and appreciate each other. I treasure the times we have together.

But You are far greater than my family, for You are my heavenly Father. You are perfect, kind, merciful, and just. Thank You for caring about and forgiving me.

You are holy. You are my Father and my God. And Your only begotten Son, Jesus Christ, who paid the ultimate sacrifice with love and mercy, is my Lord and Savior!

Your Son loved me so much, He took my sins upon His shoulders. He died and triumphed over wrong. Now, I praise You for allowing me to come directly to You in prayer.

Once, I chose to give you life through a physical birth, My child. Now, I give you a spiritual birth, through Jesus. I and My Son are One; and you, My child, are Mine.

Thank You for giving me a new life in You.

*All honor to God. . .for it is his boundless mercy
that has given us the privilege of being born again.*
1 PETER 1:3 TLB

I Love to Know You, Jesus

I praise You for being my Savior and Redeemer, Lord Jesus. Thank You for having enough love for me and all of humankind to take our sins upon Yourself.

You gave Your life on a cross made for thieves. How frightening it must have been to those present when the earth shook and huge rocks shattered. How glorious then, when people were healed. Even Christians who had died were brought back to life.

How grateful I am that You won over sin and split the thick veil in the temple from top to bottom! No longer were believers separated from the Holy of Holies. Neither does the veil keep me from coming directly to You and our Father in prayer. Death didn't keep You in its grip. Instead, You came alive after three days. Now You are in heaven with our Father.

In all my ways I exalt You, Jesus. I praise You for how You also abide in my heart. Not only are You my Savior, but You are my Friend, my Counselor, my Teacher. Thank You for changing my life. Thank You for providing hope to my descendants through Your saving grace. I commit them to You, O Lord. May they always know, love, and obey You. I love to know You, Lord. You are more than life to me.

For I know whom I have believed
and I am convinced that He is able to guard
what I have entrusted to Him until that day.

2 Timothy 1:12 nasb

Let Me Learn from You, Lord

I wrote down the lessons the computer technician taught me today and saved them, Lord. Sometimes I try to solve problems and do things the hard way without asking for Your help. Then You remind me You are here to teach me.

Let me learn Your valuable lessons, Lord. Thank You for charting my path, for instructing me when to go or stop and where to rest. Keep my heart pliable as I search for the things of You. You are my refuge and strength. You are my forever-present help in my times of need and in seeking advice.

I come to You in prayer. Help me search out the things You have for me to learn. I open my Bible and pore over Your timeless, wise words. You, Lord, are the Way, the Truth, and the Life. I constantly want to study Your lessons and store them in my heart. May I find Your approval as You guide me in understanding the Truth.

I take delight in teaching you, My child. Each day as you learn My truth, it shall free you from the bondage of this world. Call upon Me. Keep reading My Word. In turn, I will answer you and tell you great and marvelous things.

Teach me, Lord, and I will listen.

Lord, I am overflowing with your blessings,
just as you promised.
Now teach me good judgment as well as knowledge.
For your laws are my guide.
PSALM 119:65–66 TLB

You Are My Way

The garden path to Happy and Minnie Green's outhouse was a short distance but felt more like a mile, Lord. As a child, I didn't know there were outhouses until I spent a summer with this family. It wasn't bad during the daytime—lined with wildflowers, quack grass, and crickets. But my nine-year-old feet stopped in their tracks when darkness approached. Flashlight in hand, the older daughters accompanied me. Their cheerful presence and my thoughts of You helped chase scary shadows away.

As an adult, I'm not so afraid to walk in the dark now, as long as there are plenty of streetlights. But I'm often fearful of the darkness of life's uncertainties. This is one of those times, Lord. I can't see what lies around the next bend. I must make some important decisions. I'm afraid and apprehensive. Please lead and direct me. I love You with all my heart. I will trust You and not depend on my own limited comprehension. Take away my fear. Light my way. Lead me to make right choices, to do what I can and leave the rest in Your capable hands.

Fear not, dear child. I am here. I am your Light. Follow Me. You will not walk in darkness but will have My Light of life, for I am the Way.

You, Lord, I will follow.

[Jesus said,] "I am the light of the world.
He who follows Me shall not walk in darkness,
but have the light of life."

JOHN 8:12 NKJV

Thank You for Your Friendship

The most wonderful thing in all the world is knowing You, Lord, my Savior and my Friend. The Bible says a true friend stays nearer than a brother. You are that kind of friend to me. Thank You for being with me day and night.

You entered my heart and set up housekeeping. You tell me the truth, even when I don't like to hear it. You patiently counsel me in right ways. You never cause me to stray, Lord, for You do not tempt. You provide zeal for my life and help me keep a positive outlook. I discover morsels of wisdom from Your words.

When I am weary, You wrap Your arms around me and give me rest. You nourish and restore my soul. When I go through deep waters, You wade ahead and hold on to me with Your strong, firm hand. Whether I am on the mountains or in the valleys of my life, You listen to my every word and care. You are more than my Friend. You are the Lover of my soul.

Let our souls entwine as one, Lord. Come what may, help me yield and trust in You. I will cling to Your counsel and follow You. At day's end, I will rest securely in Your safekeeping, for You are my treasured Friend.

[Jesus said,] "I have called you friends,
for all things that I heard from My Father
I have made known to you.
You did not choose Me,
but I chose you and appointed you."
JOHN 15:15–16 NKJV

Let Me Touch Your Hem, Lord

This thing I'm going through, Lord, is almost beyond my endurance. I'm pressed in on all sides. No matter which way I turn, I ache with indescribable pain and cry until there are no more tears. Why must I face such things? I don't know if I can take much more.

You are my Savior, my Strength and Defender. Although I'm discouraged and afraid, I will still trust in You. Let me touch the hem of Your garment, Lord. Let me hold its threads in my fingers. Help me tie a knot in the strands and not let go of my hope in You!

Come to Me, you who are heavy laden. You are My dear child. Know for certain, there are no troubles you face that others have not gone through before you. I will take these things and make a way of escape for you. Take My yoke. Place it on your shoulders. It will not make your load heavier. I am helping you carry it so your burden will become lighter and easier. Rest upon My everlasting arms, for they are under you all the time. Here is the hem of My garment. Touch it. Feel My presence. In your weakness, know My strength and healing.

Thank You, Lord Jesus, for the hem of Your garment and for Your loving touch.

[Jesus said,] Take my yoke upon you, and learn of me;
for I am meek and lowly in heart:
and ye shall find rest unto your souls.
For my yoke is easy, and my burden is light.
MATTHEW 11:29–30 KJV

Teach Me How to Fish

*A*fter all You do for me, Lord Jesus, I want to tell everyone how glorious You are. But I'm unsure. I'm afraid. I read about the way You walked by the Sea of Galilee. You found Simon (later to be called Peter) and his brother, Andrew, fishing. You bid them to lay down their nets and follow You, asking them to attract men instead of fish. At once, the fishermen stopped what they were doing and went with You. They listened and didn't hesitate.

Remember when I was a child and my dad patiently tried to teach me to fish, Lord? He and my mother loved fishing. I attempted it but could never get past putting the worm on the hook. Then our grandsons came along. Somehow they have the touch. They cast out their lines and wiggle them a little, and the fish gravitate to them. Perhaps the ability is inherited from their great-grandparents.

Lord, I want to be a fisher of men (and women). Please teach me how. Every time I try telling others about You, I stumble over my words. No one pays attention to me. Just like when I tried catching fish, I don't have the touch. Help me, Lord. Show me how to cast out my spiritual line and draw others to You.

Jesus called out to them,
"Come, follow me!
And I will make you
fishermen for the souls of men!"
MARK 1:17 TLB

I Send You a Comforter

Thank You for Your Holy Spirit, Lord. Thank You for coming into my heart. Fill me and refill me to overflowing. Train me to reach souls for You. Help me to recall the teachings from Your Word.

When I start to tell someone about Your love, remove the fear I struggle with and replace it with Your peace of mind. Surround me with Your presence. Because I love and trust in You, I ask for You to provide the right words. Anoint my words with Your power so they won't come back hollow or meaningless. Lord, let each person I talk with hear You instead of me.

You are not alone, dear child, for My Father and I send you a Helper. He abides with you now and forever. He is the Spirit of Truth, the Holy Spirit. I and the Father and the Spirit are One, working in perfect, holy harmony.

The people who do not know Me or the Father will not recognize the Holy Spirit. But you know Him, because you have invited Me as Savior into your heart.

Thank You, dear Lord, for Your Holy Spirit. Thank You for being my Helper, my Comforter, my Strength, my Guide. Thank You for blessing my words with Your great power.

[Jesus said,] "And I will pray the Father, and He will give you another Helper, that He may abide with you forever. . . but you know Him, for He dwells with you and will be in you."
JOHN 14:16–17 NKJV

My Journey with You

I'm so excited about Your Holy Spirit filling my soul, Lord. I feel I'm about to take the most exciting trip of my life—a spiritual journey with You as my Captain. I'm anxious to serve You—anytime, anywhere. What can I do for You? How I long to be useful.

In one way, I can hardly wait. In other ways, I feel unworthy of being Your servant. I'm only a regular person. Your greatness is measureless. I don't know if I can fulfill the callings You have awaiting me. Still, I will trust and obey You. Direct me as You will, Lord.

Don't be afraid, dear child. From now on, My Holy Spirit goes with you all the time. You shall be a fisher of souls. When you are weak, I shall give you strength. When you are afraid, I shall give you courage. When you are uncertain of what to do, I shall lead you.

I will trust in You, Lord, and not fear my own frailties and limited reasoning. Remind me, I pray, not to get ahead of Your will. May my motives and actions be pure and pleasing to You. Thank You for Your Holy Spirit, Lord. I'm ready now to start my journey with You.

"As I was with Moses, so I will be with you;
I will never leave you nor forsake you."

JOSHUA 1:5 NIV

Fill Me

Fill me with Your Holy Spirit, Lord. Search my heart. See if there is anything You would make right. Know my thoughts. Renew my mind and lead me into Your everlasting ways.

Help me shed the weights that will hold me back from being a victorious and joy-filled Christian. Cleanse me with Your holy power. Wash me through and through, my Lord. Plant seeds of Your Holy Spirit within me that will produce Your love, joy, and peace of mind and heart. Grant me patience, kindness, and purity. Cause me to be faithful, no matter how difficult things become. Teach me gentleness and self-control.

Once I thought I could do all these things through my own strength of will. Now I know I am able to have these spiritual fruits only through the power of Your Holy Spirit who dwells in me. No longer am I oppressed by temptations and fears, for You are closer than life itself. You dwell within me. You crucify my sinful nature and give me victory in You. Let me keep in step with Your Spirit and synchronize my will with Yours. Thank You for filling me with Your Spirit, dear Lord. I yield my all to You.

May the God of hope fill you with all joy
and peace as you trust in him,
so that you may overflow with hope
by the power of the Holy Spirit.
ROMANS 15:13 NIV

61

How Can I Overcome?

Thinking of what my life used to be like before knowing You leaves me weary, Lord. I grieve to see others who are lost and don't know You. This sinful existence, supposedly full of fun and excitement, is only a farce—an empty mirage. It leads to sadness and ruin. Thank You for saving me from it.

Yet I face challenges. At times, sin and sorrow press in from every side, no matter which way I turn. How can I overcome these ordeals I must cope with? Give me strength enough to resist the devious temptations put before me. As I do, please let others listen to what I'm trying to tell them about You. I love You, Lord, and want to overcome these things through You.

I shall overcome, dear one. I am your Fort, your Rock, and a strong Tower to which you can run. I am like the strong horn of a mighty fighting bull. I will defend and buffer you, no matter the difficulty.

Thank You, Lord God, for Your promise that no temptation, no problem, is too great when I obey You. Thank You for helping me each time I call Your name. I praise You for empowering me with Your Holy Spirit and providing the right words when I tell others about You. In You I completely trust.

[Jesus said,] "But when the Holy Spirit has come upon you, you will receive power to testify about me with great effect. . .and to the ends of the earth."

ACTS 1:8 TLB

You Give Me Zeal

*W*here does this passion to tell everyone who will listen about Your wonderful love come from, Lord? Is it from Your Holy Spirit dwelling within me? I feel an urgency to win souls for You. Not because I think I have to. I simply long for others to experience the bountiful blessings of having You in their lives.

Like an all-encompassing, loving Friend and Counselor, You are here. You provide me with a fire and zeal that almost cause me to burst, unless I'm able to pass them on in either actions or words.

I don't know why You bless me so, dear Lord. I'm just a simple person who wants to love and serve You with all my heart. I am awed by how You give me an enthusiasm and a deep inner joy and hope, no matter what circumstances I face. As long as I focus on You and the scriptures and take my mind off the things of this world, I have hope with peace of heart and mind.

Thank You for teaching me how to be patient in facing problems, to be faithful in prayer to You during the good and bad. I praise You for keeping my fervor and zeal for You alive and well. To You, Lord, be honor and acclamation and power. Amen.

[Jesus said,]
"And behold, I am sending forth
the promise of My Father upon you;
but you are to stay in the city until you are
clothed with power from on high."
LUKE 24:49 NASB

Cling to the Vine

I want to be a blessing to everyone I'm around, Lord. A lot of times I do all right. But when I'm with people I live and work with day after day, it's a lot harder. They know my every attitude. No matter how hard I try, I can't reflect You without Your Holy Spirit working through me.

I read in my Bible that You are the Vine, and my heavenly Father is the Gardener. It also says I am one of Your branches. You grafted me to You when I became Your child. I choose to remain close to You, Lord. Thank You for pruning away the things in my life that are undesirable to You. May I please You in all my ways and bring forth spiritual fruit that comes directly from You. Please show me how.

My dear child, I abide in you, and you abide in Me. If you remain in Me, you will produce much of My fruit. Apart from Me, you are not able to yield any of it. No matter your good intentions, your efforts will be a waste. Cling to Me. Draw life from Me. And I will help you bring forth the sweet-tasting fruit of My Spirit.

I will cling to You, Lord—my Vine, the source of all that is good and holy.

[Jesus said,] "I am the vine, you are the branches.
He who abides in Me, and I in him, bears much fruit;
for without Me you can do nothing."

JOHN 15:5 NKJV

Fruit of the Holy Spirit

Once I tried to have the fruits of Your Spirit in my life by working hard to achieve them—one at a time. It didn't take long for me to realize I couldn't do it that way. Thank You for showing me this fruit comes only from Your Holy Spirit dwelling within me.

Fill me, Lord. Take my talents, my time. Bless the work of my hands. Grant me the spiritual gifts You would have me receive. More than anything, help me yield my will to Yours.

I pray for Your Spirit to work within me, dear Lord. Let me abide in You. In turn, live within my heart and direct me. Tell me where to go and what to do in accordance with Your will. Let my life be a living proof of Your presence abiding within me. Cause Your spiritual fruit to grow in abundance.

My child, I shall produce in you love, joyfulness, harmony of heart and mind, selflessness, kindheartedness, uprightness, faithfulness, sensitivity, self-control. Love Me with all your heart and your soul and your strength. When you are guided by My Holy Spirit, you will be able to do what pleases Me.

Plant the seeds of Your fruit within me, Lord. Tend the garden of my heart. Make it grow and flourish for Your glory.

But the fruit of the Spirit is love, joy, peace, longsuffering, kindness, goodness, faithfulness, gentleness, self-control. Against such there is no law.
GALATIANS 5:22–23 NKJV

How Can I Repay You?

*L*ord, I lift my heart to You in thanksgiving and praise this evening for how You were here with me today. While being faced with several problems to untangle, You showed me the answers once again. Thank You, Lord.

I glance over my prayer list from this past year and am amazed at how many petitions You answered then—just like You did today. I recall the nearly impossible challenges I faced and how You repeatedly brought me through victoriously. I feel undeserving, Lord. How can I repay You for the incredible things You do? Will serving You every hour of every day, with all the strength I can muster, make up for Your blessings? Not a chance. Will selling my worldly possessions repay You? Your blessings are priceless. I love You, Lord. Show me what I can do for You.

You need not repay Me, dear one. I merely want you to love Me with all your heart and soul and mind. Give yourself, holy and pleasing, to Me. I am the Potter. You are the clay. Allow My Spirit to fill and mold you so you can pass My love on to others. As My Father sent Me, I therefore send you.

Thank You for calling me to serve You, Lord. Let Your plans and ways be mine.

[Jesus said,] "You did not choose Me, but I chose you
and appointed you that you should go and bear fruit,
and that your fruit should remain, that whatever
you ask the Father in My name He may give you.
These things I command you, that you love one another."
JOHN 15:16–17 NKJV

Serving You with My Love

*W*ho can compare to You, dear Lord? There is no other I love more. How I treasure my times in communication with You. But I want this love I have to *do* something for You. Although You're in my heart, I can't touch or see You. How can I serve You with my love?

My child, when you give others your love, you do so as to Me. Do not be afraid to shake the hand or hug the unlovely. Imagine that person being Me. Love by feeding the hungry, and you feed Me. Offer a drink of water to the thirsty, and you do so to Me.

Lovingly open your home to someone, and you welcome Me, as well. Give your clothing to one in need, and you give it to Me

Take time from your busy days to visit the sick. Go to those in prison and tell them of My love for them. Never mind the clanging doors that slam shut behind you. You are there to help set their spirits free. Reach out and watch over the aged in rest homes. When you love all of these, you are giving love to Me.

I will serve others with love as unto You, Lord.

[Jesus said,] "For I was hungry
and you gave me something to eat,
I was thirsty and you gave me something to drink,
I was a stranger and you invited me in,
I needed clothes and you clothed me,
I was sick and you looked after me,
I was in prison and you came to visit me."
MATTHEW 25:35–36 NIV

Gentle Service

*W*hen You met with Your disciples in the upper room for the Last Supper, You already knew who would betray You, Lord Jesus. You also had foreknowledge of those who would run away and not stand their ground for You.

It's difficult comprehending the gentle love and service You expressed by washing Your disciples' feet. You didn't eliminate Judas, Lord—and certainly not Peter. In spite of the things You knew, which were most likely breaking Your heart, You still continued loving and serving.

I can visualize You getting up from the meal and wrapping a towel around Your waist. I can almost hear the sound of trickling water while You poured it into a basin. If I had been there and felt Your strong yet gentle hands washing my dirty, sandy feet and drying them with the towel, I think I would have felt overwhelmed and unworthy, much like Peter.

My first reaction would be for You not to wash my feet. I should be the one who would wait on You. Yet this was part of Your plan. Like a servant, You once bathed Your disciples' dirty feet. As a Savior, You did more for them—and me. You cleansed our dirty, sin-filled souls.

Teach me, Lord, to serve with this same unfaltering love.

So he [Jesus] got up from the supper table, . . .
poured water into a basin, and began to wash
the disciples' feet.
JOHN 13:4–5 TLB

A Living Sacrifice

I often ponder how You, Lord Jesus, are alive in heaven at the right-hand side of Your Father. I'm grateful for Your bringing my needs to Him. At the same time, Your Spirit abides in my heart. Still, I think of the price You paid to free me from sin. Thank You for dying on the cross and sacrificing Yourself for me.

What would You have me do for You, dear Lord? If I should give my life for another, it wouldn't compare to everything You have done and are doing for me.

Just follow Me, My child. Be willing to give up anything in order to serve Me. Take up the cross I have for You to carry. Deny your own desires and aspirations daily in order to accomplish what I call you to do.

Help me put Your will ahead of my own wants and desires. I know when I do, I will gain the joy and everlasting peace You offer me. I willingly dedicate my life to You, Lord. How wonderful it is to experience Your blessings and true happiness beyond measure.

Take everything in my life, Lord, and use it for Your glory.

Then Jesus said to His disciples,
"If anyone desires to come after Me,
let him deny himself, and take up his cross, and follow Me.
For whoever desires to save his life will lose it,
but whoever loses his life for My sake will find it.
For what profit is it to a man if he gains the whole world,
and loses his own soul?"
Matthew 16:24–26 nkjv

Let Me Share Your Goodness

I'm thankful, Lord, that after three days in the tomb, You didn't remain dead. Instead, You triumphed over sin and death and rose from that awful, cold grave. Before You died, You had the power to spread Your goodness everywhere You went. After You came back to life, You continued spreading kindness. Even now, You send Your Holy Spirit to help me.

That same power to do good for others and overcome the sin and sadness of this world is here for me today. Thank You, Lord Jesus, for dying and rising again for me. Thank You for the constant, helpful presence of Your Holy Spirit who dwells within me.

Grant me Your strength and unconditional love as You lead me to spread Your goodness to others. Grant me new vitality in well-doing. Make my feet swift and my hands sure. All credit belongs to You. Whatever kindness I do is only significant and has eternal value if it comes through You. Because of this, let my every word and action be acceptable in Your sight, O Lord, my vitality and my salvation.

Every good gift and every perfect gift is from above,
and comes down from the Father of lights,
with whom there is no variation or shadow of turning.
JAMES 1:17 NKJV

Teach Me Faithfulness

I just went through some depressing experiences, Father. I must be hard to get along with during these times. I felt so low, I wasn't able to think clearly. I'm sorry for the way I responded to You and others. Please forgive me. In spite of it all, I'm thankful for Your steadfast closeness.

I praise You, Father, for the wonderful ways You have shown Your faithfulness to me. Even when I'm at my lowest ebb, You are there—willing to help me. Thank You for never turning Your back, for looking for the best in me.

I'm grateful for those who have patiently stood by me through thick and thin. When I couldn't see a way through all my problems, my friends helped me sort things out. When I felt no one cared, they never deserted me. Thank You for their unwavering love and constant, selfless actions.

Show me how to be faithful like You. Help me stand by others when I may be the only one who is doing so. Grant me patience to help in whatever ways are needed, even when they are depressed, unpleasant, or lost in spirit. Remind me to look for the best in them. Teach me how to love and care for them as You do me.

A true friend is always loyal,
and a brother [or sister] is born
to help in time of need.
PROVERBS 17:17 TLB

Am I Good Enough for You?

I want to serve You, Lord. Yet I occasionally feel inadequate. Am I smart or attractive enough? Sometimes I'm awkward in words and actions. Others have more status. Many are more educated. I don't possess impressive material things. Sometimes I feel like others look down on me, as though they're much better. Perhaps they are, Lord. As I forge bravely ahead in serving You, I frequently hit a wall of negative thoughts: *I'm not good enough to really do this job well.*

Why did You call me to serve like this, Lord, when others are more capable? I know feeling this way isn't Your will. I want to heed Your call. Here I am, asking for Your help.

You must view yourself as I do, dear one. You are precious to Me. Each time you feel you are not good enough to serve Me, focus your mind, soul, and every fiber of your being on the things of Me. I am the One who calls you. I am the One who decides how capable you are of serving Me. Cast off the negative and trust in Me for help. I will have you do great things. Be filled with My Holy Spirit. I will give you power to serve.

Thank You for Your direction and confidence, Lord.

Therefore, holy brothers and sisters,
who share in the heavenly calling,
fix your thoughts on Jesus,
whom we acknowledge as our apostle and high priest.

HEBREWS 3:1 NIV

What Can I Do for Another Today?

This is a new day, Father. Let me begin it by reaching for Your guiding hand. I want to do my best for You in all I do and say. What can I do for another today? Help me be sensitive and do unnoticed things for those around me. Help me be mindful of the opportunities to show acts of courtesy while driving to my job. Let me take an extra step in sharing the workload. Most of all, remind me at day's end to especially demonstrate love to my dear family.

It's strange how these things pump energy and warmth into me, Lord. Perhaps it is the approval of Your Holy Spirit working. Even if things go wrong and events all seem uphill, still I know You have used me as Your instrument to make life a little better for those around me.

Thank You for remaining close and showing me what I can do for others today. As You and I work together, I enjoy Your loving, kind ways more. Thank You for giving Yourself to me. Thank You for showing me how to give of myself.

[Jesus said,] "These things I have spoken to you,
that My joy may remain in you,
and that your joy may be full.
This is My commandment,
that you love one another as I have loved you."
JOHN 15:11–12 NKJV

You Are Altogether Lovely

*H*ow lovely You are, O Lord. You are the order in all Your creation. You cause the mornings, the days, and the evenings to rejoice in Your presence. Mountains show Your strength. You visit the ground with rainfall and make it yield. You provide grain, fruits, and vegetables for us to eat. You pour Your rain into ridges and settle them in furrows. You slow the drops to soft, refreshing showers that bless every growing thing.

You cover each season with goodness. Somehow You work them together. Your loving-kindness blankets the forests and pastures. You bring forth flocks of birds and countless varieties of animals.

Who in heaven or earth is so full of grace and glory? Who can compare to You? There is no other so great as You, whose very presence can cause the earth to tremble or calm my troubled heart. You make rock-hard ocean waves to crash, shifting turquoise waters from steel-green to crystal clear rivulets. You also cleanse and redirect my life.

You are altogether lovely, O Lord. How marvelous the way You shower Your love upon each of us, above and beyond anything else in this world's creation. You, who rule over everything, take the time to talk with and listen to me. Thank You for the caring way You always have time for me and minister to my heart.

This is my beloved, and this is my friend.
SONG OF SOLOMON 5:16 NKJV

I Wait on You

Here I am, Lord. I need Your help. There are so many who need You. I'm stretched too thin. I can't do it all. I feel misunderstood and unappreciated. Am I seeking to do my will and not Yours? I know my vision of Your call is slipping. There is only one way I can regain it. I need to seek Your presence and wait on Your direction. In Your answer, I know I will regain the strength and confidence required.

As I pause before You, dear Lord, I enjoy Your understanding ways. Thank You for not looking down on me when I'm discouraged. Thank You for Your promise that You will renew my strength and cause me to mount up with wings like eagles. Only through Your wisdom, guidance, and power can I run and not be weary, walk and not faint.

Thank You for hearing my prayer and teaching me graciousness. You are my joy and strength. I'm grateful for Your helping me to look up, take courage, and press forward. Thank You for showering me with Your much-treasured compassion. I praise You for Your love, insight, and direction, and for giving me the good sense to wait on You and receive Your guidance.

Even the youths shall faint and be weary, and the young men shall utterly fall: But they that wait upon the LORD shall renew their strength; they shall mount up with wings as eagles; they shall run, and not be weary; and they shall walk, and not faint.

ISAIAH 40:31 KJV

More Than Enough for the Day

This has been a tight month financially, Father. Someone needed my help though. I felt You led me to take action. Thank You for providing me the faith to give above my tithe. Everything I have already belongs to You. I'm grateful for Your promise to meet my needs, and that You know them even better than I do.

You always provide what I need each day, each month. You often give me more than I need. Thank You for Your bountiful blessings and for helping me trust in You. Because of this, I'm filled with Your peace and confidence. I read how manna fell in Bible times. Just enough for each day. When the Israelites complained, You still remained with them. Like me, they sometimes learned things the hard way. You taught them patience and how to trust and depend on You.

Let me learn from their lessons. As I place my faith in You, I'm encouraged by Your promises to meet my daily needs. Like many times before, I enjoy Your benevolence, Father—"pressed down, and shaken together, and running over" (Luke 6:38 KJV). Thank You for giving me more than enough for each day.

[Jesus said,] "Give, and it will be given to you.
They [the fruits of your gifts] will pour
into your lap a good measure—
pressed down, shaken together, and running over.
For by your standard of measure
it will be measured to you in return."

LUKE 6:38 NASB

Apart with You

I steal away awhile to unwind, Lord, apart from the press of my hurried life. Here, in this quiet place, I find peace and tranquility with You. As I seek Your quiet strength, I feel You wipe worry and weariness from me. Things of this world don't matter nearly as much as the precious time we have, communing with one another.

I feel like a child sitting at Your feet. Time stops. I share with You all I've been doing—my failures and victories, fears and hopes. I sense You laugh with me over the amusing things and cry with me when I share my woes.

Here, I draw apart and rest. Here, I gain strength, lest I burn out from responsibilities I shoulder. You offer me spiritual food, the bread of life from Your Bible. Your words are sure and true. I hold them in my heart. Here, I drink from the living fountain of Your cleansing Holy Spirit. You search my heart and redirect my way. We commune as Friend with friend.

I lean back and close my eyes. I see Your face in my mind. What a sweet breakaway this is, physically and spiritually. As I focus on You, my vitality is renewed. My thoughts are set on the ways You lead me. Thank You for welcoming me to draw apart with You.

[Jesus said,]
"Come with me by yourselves to a quiet place
and get some rest."
MARK 6:31 NIV

You Calm My Fears

There are things I face in my life that cause me to be anxious, Father. They are so overwhelming, they cause me to freeze in my tracks. You are my source of strength and my Redeemer. I bring my fears to You now and cast them at Your feet. I trust in You and will not rely on my own perception. In every way, I will depend on You, for I know You go before me.

As you place your faith in Me, My child, I will cause your uprightness to shine like the noonday sun! Be quiet and calm. Do not try to run ahead of Me. Wait patiently for My will to be accomplished, for I am here to defend you and free you from worry. I am your shelter and fort. I am your ever-present Guide through your troubles.

Thank You for being with me, Father. How comforting it is to put my trust in You. Your Spirit radiates infinite hope deep into my heart. Thank You for watching over me and those I love. Even when my faith is minuscule, You are enough, for You are my Lord. You are my strength, the source of my song. Through all these things, You give me joy. Thank You for replacing my fears with faith in You.

When I am afraid,
I put my trust in you.
In God, whose word I praise—
in God I trust
and am not afraid.
Psalm 56:3–4 niv

A Mother's Prayer

*F*ather, I bring my children and my children's children to You today. Bless and watch over them, I pray. Things are troubling and unsure in this world. Sometimes I shudder at what could possibly happen to my family. Will they live to grow old? Will they love and serve You all the days of their lives?

I know You love my children and grandchildren as much and more than I am capable of doing. Although they are part of me, they belong to You. I believe You prayed for them in the Garden of Gethsemane before You were taken to the cross. They were purchased by You with the price of Your life. As I dedicate them to You, I trust Your promise to keep them in Your care.

Take heart, dear mother. If any of your offspring should soar to the highest heavens or go below the deepest sea, I shall be there with them. I will be with them in the darkest and lightest hours. Nothing can keep Me from loving your children. Each time I hear them pray, I bring their concerns to the throne of My heavenly Father.

Thank You, Father, for answering my prayer. Thank You for Your love that goes beyond time and space.

The LORD bless thee, and keep thee:
The LORD make his face shine upon thee,
and be gracious unto thee:
The LORD lift up his countenance upon thee,
and give thee peace.
NUMBERS 6:24–26 KJV

Key to the Unknown

I know not what the future holds, dear Lord, but I'm sure You hold the key. I'm glad You are the One who cares for my days ahead. If they were in my hands, I would probably make a mess of things. How wonderful it is that You are all-knowing. Your insight and wisdom surpass everything else.

Thank You for unlocking the door to each day as it comes my way. I take great comfort and joy in how You step through that door before me. Then You guide me through. I don't have the foresight to make life's decisions without Your counsel. You give me security with each step I take.

When things become a fog and I grope in a mist of confusion, I feel Your sure hand taking hold of mine and leading me. You know my wants and my needs. You understand my greatest concerns. When I become anxious about the future, You turn the key again. Patiently, You unlock the door to faith and help me trust in You.

Thank You, Lord, for holding the answers to the unknown. As I walk this road of life, I look back and understand a little how You have fit things together for my good. My past, my present, and my future, I place in Your capable hands.

For I know the thoughts that I think toward you,
says the LORD, thoughts of peace and not of evil,
to give you a future and a hope.
Then you will call upon Me and go and pray to Me,
and I will listen to you.
JEREMIAH 29:11–12 NKJV

Your Assurance

Thank You, Father God, for giving me Your blessed assurance that I am in Your constant watch—not only me, but everything and everyone I care about. Thank You for helping me to lay my entire life on Your altar. Thank You for helping me remember how much You love me.

In full assurance of Your love, I relinquish my guilt and pain. In full assurance, I know You roll it all away. You remove my bitterness. You comfort me. You cover my tears with Your smile. In the desert scenes of my life, Your hope bursts forth like vibrant cactus flowers blooming after a sudden rain shower.

When my days go as smooth as glass, I praise You for Your assuring love. When the storms of life crash in and billows roar, I still praise You. You are always near—guiding and watching over me. When I'm at my best, I sense Your approval. When I'm at my worst, I experience Your love and forgiveness.

Here with You, I leave it all, my hopes and dreams and wants. Here, I trust Your assuring hands to pick up this struggling life of mine, turn it around, then mold it in the way You know is best. I give my all to You because of the calm assurance You place within me.

*"The LORD himself goes before you
and will be with you; he will never leave you
nor forsake you."*

DEUTERONOMY 31:8 NIV

I Come to Your Fountain

*F*ather, occasionally I face so many demands that I don't know which way to turn. I frequently pour everything I have to offer into other people and situations, and I go beyond my abilities. This is one of those times, Lord. I'm so burned out, I don't want to talk with anyone or go anywhere. I need to come away with You.

Here I am in this quiet place. The world goes on around me. But all is calm in my secret spot of worship. No one knows I'm here but my understanding husband. Hear me, O Lord, as I share my heart and mind with You. Thank You for identifying with my every concern. I recognize Your voice speaking to my heart. How I love Your calming words. I open my Bible and ask for guidance. The answers jump off the page and minister to me. I dive into Your spiritual living fountain. You wash away my unwanted attitudes. You soothe my anxious mind. The presence of Your Holy Spirit wraps around me like a comforting blanket. Here, I rest and feel secure. I drink from Your well that never runs dry. You pump new energy and joyfulness into me. You replace my defeated mindset with Your revitalizing presence.

Thank You for Your spiritual living fountain. Thank You for restoring my soul.

For you are the Fountain of life;
our light is from your light.
PSALM 36:9 TLB

You Are My Yokefellow

Thank You for this calling You give me, Lord. Although it's a huge undertaking, You furnish the answer to lightening my load. It's simply working hand in hand with You. Your Bible says to take Your yoke upon me, because Your yoke is easy and light. When I first read this, Lord, I wondered how taking on more of a burden could be better. Then You helped me understand.

I read how long ago two people shared a yoke placed upon their shoulders. The yoke helped make them stronger while they carried their load and worked together. Even machinery works this way. Why should this calling from You bring worry when You are offering to help me?

Now I put on Your yoke, Lord, and we work as one. Thank You for taking control and leading me. You are my Yokefellow, my Guide, my Helper. How I enjoy working with You, rather than charging off my own way. Should I tend to stray, please tug me back on the right path.

Thank You for Your gentle commands and sure precepts. I take pleasure in Your being with me. Thank You for how Your hand, the same capable hand that bore creation, still guides and helps me. What joy we share as we work as one!

[Jesus said,] "Come to Me, all who are weary and heavy-laden, and I will give you rest."
MATTHEW 11:28 NASB

Your Healing Whisper

*M*y mind is tangled with the cares of the day as I come to You, O Lord. I praise You for Your healing whispers of love and encouragement. In You I find freedom from strife. I wait on Your strengthening presence. In You I find safety, peace of mind. You help me to lay aside my trials. I fix my heart on Your encouraging words of hope.

I come to You and listen to Your teachings. You are so gentle. In You I find quietness and confidence. In You I find strength and inner peace. You heal my emotional scars as You teach me to forgive and let go.

You replace my wounds with wellness. I praise You for working wonderful miracles in me. You are my Shepherd. You are the One who makes me whole—physically, spiritually, and emotionally. Thank You for granting me relief in my days of trouble—for showing me a way through. Thank You for providing me rest and for drying my tears and helping me see things clearly, allowing me to choose Your righteous ways. You are my Lord, my God. Your whispers give me confidence and teach me what is best. My soul finds healing in You, O Lord. How good You are to me.

This is what the Sovereign LORD,
the Holy One of Israel, says:
"In repentance and rest is your salvation,
in quietness and trust is your strength."
ISAIAH 30:15 NIV

A Brand-New Start

*P*raise You, Father, for Your unwavering love. Your patience with me goes beyond my comprehension. Thank You for how You have forgiven my wrongs and shown me Your steadfast compassion. Even though the sins of our ancestors can go down to the third and fourth generations, I'm grateful for Your making them stop here. This is only possible as I turn my heart and my will completely over to You. Thank You for helping me make a brand-new start.

Each day as I walk with You, I experience Your caring about my every need and concern. Nothing is too great or small for me to bring to You. When I am at my best, I know Your love. When I'm down and not pleasant to be around, You never leave me. Instead, I praise You for remaining close and comforting me. I'm thankful, Lord, that I can be completely open with You about how I feel. I'm amazed at how You never make me feel guilty when I pour out my cares to You.

Thank You for always looking for the best in me and helping me grow in the right ways. I praise You, Father, for giving me a brand-new start.

His compassions fail not.
They are new every morning;
great is Your faithfulness.
"The LORD is my portion," says my soul,
"Therefore I hope in Him!"
LAMENTATIONS 3:22–24 NKJV

Your Compassion

You are so loving and compassionate, Lord. You are a Father to me. You know me better than I know myself. Your tenderness and mercy follow me each day. Oh, how I enjoy the loving-kindness You show me. I will never forget Your bountiful blessings. I praise You for Your protecting presence.

I'm grateful for the way You go before me along life's path. You make Your ways known to me. As long as I follow Your lead, You help me not to stumble and fall. Day and night, You watch over me. When I'm awake, You are near. When I fall asleep, You surround me with Your presence. When evil or harm threatens, You spread Your wings over my trembling being, like an eagle does over its young. When I become weary and call on You for help, You carry me on Your wings and rejuvenate my soul.

Mere words cannot express my gratefulness for Your endless compassion. You, dear Father, are the One who snatched me from sin's horrible destruction. How wonderful, the way Your presence is here for me all the time. You never tire from watching over and caring for me. Thank You, dear Father. I love You so.

Praise the LORD, my soul,
and forget not all his benefits. . . .
As a father has compassion on his children,
so the LORD has compassion on those who fear him.
PSALM 103:2, 13 NIV

Your Holy Spirit Helps Make Things Right

The joy and serenity I receive from You are my source of strength, O Lord. Thank You for stirring up goodness and peace within me through the presence of Your Holy Spirit. In the back of my mind, all day long, I think of You. Scriptures and songs of praise flow through my thoughts and make my heart glad. I thank You for how wonderful You are.

My praise continually lifts to You in silent communion while I fulfill my duties. *"Do this; don't do that,"* I hear You caution. How marvelous You are in the way You care for and lead me. How I rejoice in You, Lord. How happy You make me in all circumstances. You are the awesome God of my salvation. I rejoice when good things happen. Yet even in heartache, You pour into my soul Your comforting balm of peace and joy. When trials come or problems confront me, You help me to remain capable. How amazing, the way You ease and clear my mind.

You, O Holy Spirit, are everything to me. You are the sure One I can fix my mind on. You are the answer to my concerns and needs. Over and over, I marvel at how You work and help make things right.

Trust in the LORD with all your heart, and do not rely on your own insight. In all your ways acknowledge him, and he will make straight your paths.

PROVERBS 3:5–6 RSV

The Hollow of Your Hand

When storms of life toss me about, Lord, like a bobbing cork at sea, and raging billows hide any hint of welcoming shelter, I take heart at being securely planted in the hollow of Your hand. When discouraging dark clouds glower, fearful lightning pierces, and thunderous troubles pound, I find comfort hiding in the hollow of Your strong hand.

When temptation attempts to lure me and seeks to drive me from Your path, I feel Your firm grip. There, I cling to the hollow of Your hand. When endless toil drains my energy to nothing and whirlwind challenges cause my head and emotions to spin out of control, I experience Your presence. You wrap Your steady fingers around mine and hold me in the hollow of Your hand. When I see light at the end of my troubled tunnel and take pleasure in sunshiny days, I rejoice. Still, I nestle in the hollow of Your hand.

When the time comes for life's journey to take a new turn and my earthly existence starts to ebb, I will glance back and praise You for the many times You held me close in the hollow of Your hand. When I walk the valley from death to eternal life, I will have no fear, for You shall be with me, holding me in the hollow of Your hand.

Nevertheless I am continually with You;
You hold me by my right hand.
You will guide me with Your counsel,
and afterward receive me to glory.
PSALM 73:23–24 NKJV

Your Heavenly Presence

Although I love this earthly life You provide for me, dear Lord, I yearn to enter the courtyard of Your heavenly home. There I will get to meet You face-to-face. I wonder how I will even be able to gaze upon Your beauty and holiness. I will only be able to do so through Your love and saving grace. I can't even imagine what it will be like. Oh, how I look forward to being with You, my risen Lord and Savior. You, the Lamb of God, sitting at the right hand of our heavenly Father.

When I someday awaken in heaven, my longing for the things of You will be completely fulfilled. No more will I hunger and thirst for Your awesome presence, for You will be with me all the time, for all eternity. There, You will welcome me and wrap me in Your loving arms. You will take away my pain and sorrow. You will wipe away my tears. You will feed me from Your very own table and give me drink from Your rivers of endless gladness.

In the meantime, I know I have work to do for You. So I will enjoy Your loving presence every day here on earth.

*"For the Lamb in the center of the throne
will be their shepherd, and will guide them
to springs of the water of life;
and God will wipe every tear from their eyes."*

REVELATION 7:17 NASB

I Will Meditate on You

*T*he sun creeps a little higher, removing shadows from the trail I hiked up. Dew disappears from the grass around my feet. An energetic robin calls out signals to another. Although its song isn't meant for me, I can almost hear her exhorting, "God loves *you*! God loves *you*!" During this time with You, my mind wanders to the duties awaiting me. I find myself already organizing each one. I want to keep my heart fixed on You. Please help me, Lord.

As I meditate on You, I want to let everything else go. How quickly the hour is passing. I turn my thoughts to You and pray for You to heed my prayers. Hear my voice this morning, O Lord. I look to You for Your help and guidance. I recognize Your nearness, for I know You, my God, my King. There is no other greater than You.

Cast away all else, My child. All you hear from Me is wise and perfect. Listen to Me speak to your heart. My testimony is sure. My advice will bring wisdom to you and make difficulties become simple. Everything I tell you is right. Obey Me, and you will find rejoicing in your heart.

May my thoughts, my attitudes, my words and actions be pleasing to You, O Lord, my Helper and my Savior.

*I will meditate on Your precepts
and regard Your ways.
I shall delight in Your statutes;
I shall not forget Your word.*
PSALM 119:15–16 NASB

I Will Wait on You

*L*ord, there are many things in my life I want to simply jump in and take care of—right now. I hear You advising me. Yet it's still hard to wait for Your timing and direction. Help me to be patient and listen to You.

Teach me to wait on You and receive Your encouragement. Here, I linger in prayer. Here, I seek Your bidding. Prepare me, O Lord, for what lies ahead. Strengthen me. Yes, Lord, I shall wait and obey! Enable my thoughts to become Your thoughts. Let my ways adhere to Yours.

Those who patiently linger and seek Me are greater than the rulers of mighty nations. When you wait, I shall rekindle your strength and wisdom, and carry you on My wings like a baby eagle. So refrain from launching off on your own, dear one. Stay close. Let Me help you to run, and you will not grow weary; to walk, and you will not feel faint. As you do, I will shower My mercy upon you. Each and every day, I will give you hope and certainty. Remain in prayer, and trust in Me.

Lord, here I linger, let go, and place my confidence in You.

But they that wait upon the LORD
shall renew their strength;
they shall mount up with wings as eagles;
they shall run, and not be weary;
and they shall walk, and not faint.
ISAIAH 40:31 KJV

Your Cleansing Power

*L*ord, I know there are things in my life that aren't acceptable to You. How I long to please You in every way. I realize I can do so only through the strength of Your Holy Spirit.

I come to You with an open heart. Though my sins are as scarlet, I pray for You to make them white as snow. Though my life is soiled like crimson, please cleanse me. Make me pure as spotless wool.

Walk through every room of my heart, Lord. Take the books, the movies, even my thoughts that are offensive. Here and now, I release them all to You. Help me remove and replace these with what is good, uplifting, and pure. Here and now, I allow You to sweep out the hidden dust bunnies of resentments and jealousies and replace them with Your love and forgiveness.

You give Me joy, dear child, when you open your heart to Me! Listen while I teach you My holy ways and help you walk in My truth. My cleansing power working within you will cause guilt and frustration to be gone. In their place, I will restore to you the delight of My salvation. My Holy Spirit will fill you with true happiness and peace of mind.

My heart I yield to You, Lord, in joyful anticipation.

Create in me a new, clean heart, O God,
filled with clean thoughts and right desires. . . .
Restore to me again the joy of your salvation,
and make me willing to obey you.
PSALM 51:10, 12 TLB

Rest Awhile

*I*t's the end of another full day. Here I am, sitting by a tree in our backyard. Grant me time with You. I want to relax and enjoy Your encouraging presence, Father.

I've been pushing myself too hard lately. I'm tired at night and when I awaken in the morning. The harder I work, the more I spin my wheels, trying to keep up. I feel like I'm burning out in my service for You. Please help me.

Lord, I come to You to rest awhile. You are my Shepherd. You give me everything I need. I stretch out on the cool, sweet grass. I gaze through the branches of the trees and look to the light blue sky. I sense You watching over me and providing the time-out I so badly need.

Drink in My presence while I restore your weary soul, My child. You will not burn out in serving Me as long as you obey My will. Worry not about meeting the expectations of others. Take, instead, a gentle, humble spirit and rest your soul. Accept My yoke. Allow Me to help you carry your load so your burden will become lighter. I will show you how to eliminate unnecessary things and make your steps purposeful, ordered by Me. Relax awhile. Just rest.

Ah. Thank You, Father. I'll rest and learn from You.

[Jesus said,] "Come to me,
all you who are weary and burdened,
and I will give you rest."
MATTHEW 11:28 NIV

Your Nourishment

*H*ere I am at Bible study in a friend's home, Lord. Everyone in our group is going through some struggles. You know each one well. Although it's been a day of work, I now sense Your Holy Spirit nourishing and satisfying my spiritual hunger. Help me learn from Your wise scriptures. Feed my eager soul, I pray. Grant me energy, and help me to be an encourager for my friends.

You are my God, dear Lord. How I treasure the time we have together, receiving Your blessings and love. What wonderful lessons You provide to meet our daily needs. In this little home Bible study, You give us a holy sanctuary.

Recognize My power and glory, My child. Be refreshed and experience My loving-kindness, which is better than life itself. I am the Bread of Life. Dig into the Bible verses of My Word. Feast from My nourishing teachings until you are full. Be encouraged and rejuvenated. Be blessed. Look to tomorrow with enthusiasm, wholeheartedly working as you are doing so for Me. Believe in Me. Go out. Let My words flow through and out of you so others may also know Me and experience My love.

Thank You for nourishing me to the full with Your life-giving Word.

*Then Jesus declared,
"I am the bread of life.
Whoever comes to me will never go hungry,
and whoever believes in me will never be thirsty."*
JOHN 6:35 NIV

Quietness and Confidence Are My Strength

*S*tresses of this world constantly flurry around me. I'm often confronted with discord. Some of these things don't have to do with me directly, Lord, but people come to me for help. I used to dive in and get involved with the problems. Now I'm learning to stop, pray about them, and place my trust in You. Right now, I'm faced with one of those situations. Once again, I bring an anxious concern to You in prayer.

I lay my requests before You, Lord. I rest on the promises of Your Word that You care for me and those I pray for. Then I stand back and watch You work; for through quietness and confidence in You, I find strength and direction. There is no greater problem solver than being able to bring my needs to You in prayer. Because You hear my prayers and care, I trust in You.

Fear not, My child, and be not shaken. Remain calm. Rely on Me. I will keep you in perfect peace when your mind remains on Me. Keep your heart right with Me, and I shall produce fruits of calmness and assurance and peace of mind in you, no matter what circumstances you face. Know that all things are possible with Me.

I will trust in You, Lord, and remain calm. These needs I place in Your care.

"You will keep him in perfect peace,
whose mind is stayed on You, because he trusts in You.
Trust in the LORD forever."
ISAIAH 26:3–4 NKJV

Never Too Busy

*F*ather, I feel my life is jam-packed. New projects, more classes, and meetings make me cringe. Thankfully, my schedule is easier than it used to be.

I think back on the days when our children were growing up. I loved it, Father, but it really kept me hopping. Sometimes we had children in four different schools. Extracurricular activities caused me to often put on my "supermom" cape. Our calendar looked like a little bird had tracked across every date; it was so packed with scheduled events. Later, when I worked two jobs, I came up with every time-saving method I could conjure. Still, in every stage of my life, You make time for me.

It's near the end of another school year with much to do, Father. I feel my time with You slipping. Help me to put You first and never be too busy for You.

Take time to wait on Me each day, My child, and allow Me to show you My ways. I am always here, ready and waiting to meet with you. Follow Me. I can give hours to your days.

Thank You, Father, for never being too busy for me. Here I am. Meeting with You surpasses all else.

Cause me to hear Your lovingkindness in the morning,
for in You do I trust;
cause me to know the way in which I should walk,
for I lift up my soul to You.

Psalm 143:8 nkjv

I Give My Heart to You

I give my heart to You, Lord God. I trust in You. I allow You to lead me in Your truth. Teach me. No matter where I go or who I am around, I will never be ashamed of being Your child. You are the God of my salvation. You are the One who has loved me since before the beginning of time. You are the One who showers me with tender mercies and kindness all the days of my life. Your love has no beginning or end.

Here, I wholeheartedly come to You. Here, You welcome me and listen to my prayers. How grateful I am for the love You give. With all my might, I will follow Your ways of goodness and uprightness. With all my mind and heart, I will listen while You teach me everlasting wisdom and truthfulness; for Your paths are firm and certain.

Will you always honor Me, My child? Will you always give Me your heart? Turn your face toward Me. In so doing, you gain the secret of how you can obtain true, unconditional, everlasting happiness. Follow Me, and your spirit shall prosper. Pass on My teachings to your children and your children's children. Trust in Me. No matter what, keep trusting! When you do, you shall be blessed through generations.

Yes, Lord, I shall always follow You. I give You my heart, my all.

To You, O LORD,
I lift up my soul.
O my God, in You I trust.
PSALM 25:1–2 NASB

Changing Brokenness to Beauty

*F*ather, I am broken from the things that have happened in my past. I feel as though my life was shattered in a million irreparable fragments. I am so disconnected that I'm unable to offer You anything of value in my life.

How can You help a lost cause like me, Father? Am I beyond repair?

Come to Me, My dear child. Let Me wrap My comforting arms around you. Allow Me to hug the little girl within you. Here, I hold you close, rocking you as a loving parent does a crying child. I will listen as you pour out all your bad memories. As you tell Me each one, give it to Me and do not take it back. I have broad shoulders. I can carry them all.

Yield to Me while I heal your hurts. Let Me take the fragments of your life and carefully piece them together into a beautiful new pattern. It will be one that glows with enthusiasm and joy and hope. Even life's fractures will sparkle like streaks of gold from My glorious victories. Be healed. Allow Me to replace every part of your new life with a joy that will not be squelched.

Thank You, Father, for turning my brokenness into beauty for You.

The LORD is close to the brokenhearted
and saves those who are crushed in spirit. . . .
Great is our Lord and mighty in power;
his understanding has no limit.
PSALMS 34:18; 147:5 NIV

I Will Let Go and Press Forward

*L*ord, I think back on my life and have many regrets. Why did I wait so long to follow You? Had I turned to You sooner, I wouldn't have made so many terrible mistakes. I am so sorry, Lord. In the time I have left on this earth, I want to somehow make up for those wasted years. How can I do this?

Teach me to let go of the past and leave it behind me. I realize there is only one way to look. That is forward! I come to You, ready to serve when You bid. Teach me to stretch forward to the things of You that lie ahead. Give me the prize of Your Spirit-filled calling, dear Lord—a call to tell everyone I know about Your unlimited love.

Shove out the negative thoughts of what you left behind, dear one. Think on the good things, for I bestow you with a living hope for the future. I bestow you with an inheritance that shall never perish. Make ready your heart and mind for action. Grow and mature in Me. Walk the same walk alongside Me. Be of the same mind as Me. Exercise self-control. Set your hopes completely on My grace. Let Me lead, dear one! Press on.

I look forward with great anticipation to a future with You.

One thing I do,
forgetting what lies behind and
straining forward to what lies ahead,
I press on toward the goal for the prize of
the upward call of God in Christ Jesus.
PHILIPPIANS 3:13–14 RSV

I Am Not Alone

*F*ather's Day is one of my favorite times of the year, Lord. I love taking this opportunity to do something special for my husband, my dad, and my father-in-law. Thank You for them and the love they show me. Watch over them each day. Grant them wisdom and strength so they can be useful to You.

I don't know of anything more challenging than being parents and family patriarchs. How can we always set a good example? This is a twenty-four-hour undertaking, Lord. No matter how we try, we aren't able to do it all right. Please help them.

I pray for each of these dads and our grown sons who are parents to seek Your guidance and depend on You. May they trust in You to help solve their problems. May they look to You, Lord Jesus, and Your Father and follow Your example.

My Father in heaven is a Father, too, dear one. He knows exactly how every human parent feels. They are not alone in their struggles. Know for sure I am always with them through every stage of the children's growing years, on into adulthood. I will continue to be there for them down through the generations.

Thank You, Lord, for understanding us as parents. Thank You for helping and leading these ones I love all through their years.

As a father has compassion on his children,
so the LORD has compassion on those who fear him.
PSALM 103:13 NIV

I Will Be Your Example

I want to live Your example, Lord, yet reflecting You before my family in every area of my life seems impossible. I want my actions to speak louder than anything I say. Show me how to gain their respect by my honoring You—how to treat them fairly so they don't become discouraged or bitter. Remind me to consider their needs. Help me to be honest, rather than resorting to manipulation. How I want to show them Your love.

Do not fear, dear parent. I am with you, even when things go wrong. Let Me reveal to you the way. Choose Me as the head of your home. Study and memorize My teachings in your Bible. Treasure them in your heart. Place them on your doors and walls. Teach them to your offspring while you go here and there, when you prepare to rest at night, and when you awaken in the morning. Make them a vital part of your everyday life.

Love your family unselfishly, as I do you. Show your pride and appreciation for them often. Look at these lively young sprouts around your table and see My blessings!

Thank You, Lord, for helping me live Your example, especially for my family.

Write them [the scriptures] on the doorframes of your houses and on your gates, so that your days and the days of your children may be many.
DEUTERONOMY 11:20–21 NIV

101

My Needs

*L*ord, I bring a special need to You. This thing I'm asking for may not seem important to others, but it means a lot to me. I know You understand me well, and You recognize my heart. I'm not asking for selfish reasons. I need Your help.

Place a calm assurance within me of Your loving care. No matter how You answer my request, Lord, I will trust in Your wisdom and upright foresight. I know You cherish me more than anyone else does. You created me. You recognize the depths of my heart. I believe You will answer my prayer in view of my concerns and what is best for me.

Do not fret over what will come, My child. Simply trust in Me and do good. Take delight in walking in My ways, and I shall answer the desires of your heart according to what I know is best. Be still. Wait on Me. As you commit everything to Me and trust completely in My wise decisions, I will cause your righteousness to shine like the bright morning sun. Your willingness to obey Me will beam like summer at noontime! Seek first My kingdom and righteousness, and I shall bless you beyond measure.

Above all, Lord, I set my heart on the things of You.

Commit your way to the LORD;
trust in him and he will do this:
He will make your righteous reward shine like the dawn,
your vindication like the noonday sun.

PSALM 37:5–6 NIV

Removing the "Not"

*L*ord, I'm excited about the wonderful things You do in my life. Each day is a new adventure with You by my side. How awesome it is to sense You nudging me to do this or that for You. Every time You speak to my heart, I feel Your encouraging presence. No matter what is going on in this world, You have a marvelous way of changing the "not" in my life to "can."

When others ask me how to find this joy You give me, I try to tell them. How can I help them see, so they, too, can experience this positive Christian life?

You have already taken the first step in helping them, dear one, by bringing them to Me in prayer. You have answers to your prayers because you ask. Behold, I am knocking at the door of their hearts.

Let the light of your life shine before others so they may see Me in you and give glory to My Father in heaven. In this way, they, too, will seek the joy and positive ways of My salvation.

Thank You, Lord, for how good You are. Thank You for removing the "not" from my life and replacing it with "I can, through You." Surround me with Your presence. Let Your light of positive Christianity shine through me to others.

[Jesus said,] "Don't hide your light!
Let it shine for all;
let your good deeds glow for all to see,
so that they will praise your heavenly Father."
MATTHEW 5:15–16 TLB

103

I Think on Your Goodness

How wonderful is the goodness You shower upon me, Lord. There's no way I can begin to know all the blessings You give me. How I adore You.

I think on Your kindness and tuck Your ways deep into the corners of my heart. Each day I wait on You. You make me as sturdy as a cedar planted near the water. My love and trust in You shall not be moved, because I fix my thoughts on You. Let me bear Your spiritual fruit and remain fresh and green like a well-watered orchard all the days of my life.

Your praise is music to My ears, dear child. Continue to think on the love I bestow upon you in the morning and on the faithfulness I show each night. Keep noticing what I do for you by the works of My hands. My actions are more excellent than those of any other. My hopes and dreams for you go beyond your comprehension.

I will continually seek Your mercy, Lord. How can I repay You for all You do for me? It can only be by my love. Through Your goodness, You provide for my needs. Through Your power, You give me victory over temptations and troubles. I want to tell everyone of Your deep compassion. To You I give all glory and praise!

*What shall I render to the LORD
for all His benefits toward me?
I shall lift up the cup of salvation
and call upon the name of the LORD.*
PSALM 116:12–13 NASB

104

I Will Let You

*F*ather, I just talked with my friend. You know who she is. When she shares her worries with me regarding her grown child, she weeps. Her son is making some disastrous decisions.

I share her sadness. I've known this family since their son was a little boy. If he doesn't turn his heart over to You and change, his actions may cause him to suffer for the rest of his life.

We prayed together and hugged. Again, she gave her grown child to You and placed him in Your care. We know You love him even more than any of us is capable of doing.

Along with trusting You, Father, I'm asking for You to calm my friend through Your assurances.

I do care, My child—not only for you, but for your friend and her son. Listen to Me and be comforted; and I will comfort her as well. You and your friend belong to Me. So does this young man I love so dearly. I will handle this situation in My own way and in My own time. All you need to do during these trials is keep your faith in Me. Trust Me. Obey Me completely. Let go, and let Me do the rest.

I will, Father. Thank You for helping my friend to let go and let You.

[Jesus said,] "Believe in God;
believe also in me. . . .
Do not let your hearts be troubled
and do not be afraid."
JOHN 14:1, 27 NIV

I Shall Wait on You

Thank You for teaching me to trust You, Lord. When I do, You help my faith to become strong. I praise You for abiding with me all the time. Day after day, You surround me and the loved ones I pray for. Every moment, You protect me from evil and harm. I shall depend on You above all else.

When wrongdoers are up to no good, You replace my fear with faith. I know fretting only causes harm, so I will trust You and obey. No matter what, I praise Your holy name. I continually feed on Your scriptures and take delight in Your ways.

It is good for you, dear child, to pray that your loved ones will follow Me. Because of your trust in Me, I shall cause the faith within you to grow beyond measure. Yes, I regard the desires of your heart. Fear not. I am honoring your prayers, for those who wait on Me, I bless.

Thank You for keeping Your hand on the ones I pray for and not giving up on them, Lord. Thank You for talking to their hearts, coaxing them to follow You. How I praise You. Those I love are Yours, Lord. I shall wait on You and rest in Your care.

Trust in the Lord with all your heart
and do not lean on your own understanding.
In all your ways acknowledge Him,
and He will make your paths straight.

Proverbs 3:5–6 nasb

Victory over Defeat

$\mathcal{L}$ ord, these things You call me to do are enormous in my eyes. I don't know if I can do well enough to gratify You. What if I fail? I want to obey You. I want You to be pleased with my serving You. Remove my fear of defeat, Lord. I will do my best, then ask for You to take over. Grant me the ability, wisdom, and energy to do this for Your glory.

I look to You, Lord. It is from You that my help comes. You are the One who made heaven and earth. You are the One who hears me and is helping with my needs right now. It isn't by my might or power that these things are accomplished, but by Your Spirit.

What I call you to do may not be accomplished the way you envision or even see as successful; nonetheless, it will be according to My will. When I call you and you obey Me, there is no such thing as defeat. I bless even through failures, so fear not. I am the Lord, your God. I see the bigger picture. Trust in Me. For you, whom I call, are the apple of My eye.

I will follow You, Lord. I will not fear failure or defeat. In You I find victory.

And the Spirit of the Lord shall rest upon him,
the Spirit of wisdom, understanding, counsel and might;
the Spirit of knowledge and of the fear of the Lord.
His delight will be obedience to the Lord.

Isaiah 11:2–3 TLB

In Danger

*L*ord, I'm in danger! I must keep my head and not let fear cloud my judgment. Even though I am afraid, I trust in You. Please help me. Watch over me and keep me safe. Be with my loved ones, Lord, and protect them.

Because You are my refuge and strength, I'm learning to cast my fear on You; for You are my help, always present in times of danger and trouble. I know You are with me, so I trust and depend on You. In You, Lord, all things are possible.

Your Bible promises that should the earth shake and crack, or the mountains fall into the sea, or the floodwaters roar and foam, You are here watching over me. Should evil attempt to assault me or dangers cross my path, You are here, surrounding me.

I am your help, My child. I am the One who sustains you. I am the One who delivers you. Each time you call upon Me for protection, I summon My angels to circle and deliver you. I am your shield and fortress. Fear not the terrors by night nor the dangers you may face in a day. I am always with you. I shall never leave or forsake you.

I will trust in You, dear Lord. I will hide beneath Your wings and not be afraid.

God is our refuge and strength,
a very present help in trouble.
Therefore we will not fear.

PSALM 46:1–2 NASB

Certainty in an Uncertain World

*A*nxieties press in from every side these days, Father. Children see and hear things they should not. Adults are forced to deal with overwhelming problems because of our sin-sick world. There are wars and rumors of wars, earthquakes and fires, floods and tornadoes. Even nature's balance seems strange.

Our high-technology lifestyle makes our everyday world so complex that the most brilliant people have trouble keeping up. Where does that leave our disabled and elderly? What about our children and grandchildren? What is their future, Father? Where is the certainty of life in this uncertain world?

I am here for those who turn to Me and follow My ways. No matter what is going on in life, it is nothing new. I have always been here for those who belong to Me. As I was with Moses centuries ago, I am still by your side, leading and helping you. Be certain you are My child. I shall also be here for your children, on down through the generations as you trust and obey My precepts. I will by no means leave or disown you. Fear not, dear one. I am your certainty.

My heart is fixed on You, Father. I refuse to be bogged down by uncertainty. Instead, I will follow and trust You.

Show me your ways, LORD, teach me your paths;
guide me in your truth and teach me, for you are God
my Savior, and my hope is in you all day long.
PSALM 25:4–5 NIV

Today was just average, Father. But something was missing. My steps felt heavy. Now I'm home and can take time to reflect. I realize I've carried discouragement with me through my whole day. In Your Word, as always, I find my answers.

When I'm discouraged, I can bring You my cares and cast them at Your feet. Tonight I will fix my thoughts on You and Your capable ways. I won't allow myself to fret over life's circumstances. Thank You, my Father, for promising in the Bible to care for me and my concerns. I'm glad I can claim these promises as my own. Thank You for helping me drop this discouragement. I've been lugging it like a shabby, heavy suitcase filled with worries. Thank You for Your warm, hope-filled presence.

Yes, I care for you. You are My child. You carry the name of My Son, Jesus Christ, for you are a Christian. I am always here to help you during good and bad times. Take heart, and do not be discouraged. Take joy in My sustenance and love. Press forward. Keep doing the work I have called you to do. I am with you every step of the way.

Praise You, my Father, for providing me with hope and encouragement. Thank You for giving me just enough for each day.

"Fear not, for I am with you; be not dismayed,
for I am your God. I will strengthen you, yes, I will help you,
I will uphold you with My righteous right hand."

Isaiah 41:10 nkjv

You Care

*L*ord, I have some huge needs. I'm in want not only for my physical well-being, but for relief from relentless amounts of stress I am forced to cope with. I don't see how it is possible for my hardships to be overcome. Everything seems so hopeless.

Does anyone care about what I'm going through? There must be someone. I know You do, Lord. But I ask for Your assurance that You are here, working things out and helping me through all these trials. Please minister to me, I pray. Meet my needs. Encourage my soul. Speak to me, Lord, and shower me with Your care.

I am your refuge, My dear one. I will provide for you each day. Simply trust in Me. I see your heart and hear your cries. I will help you through these troublesome times. In order for Me to do so, you must be determined to seek first My kingdom and My righteousness. See the birds outside your window? I tend them. And I certainly look after you. Give your worries and troubles to Me, for I care for you.

I will trust in You, Lord. Thank You for loving me and watching over for me.

The LORD is good,
a refuge in times of trouble.
He cares for those who trust in him.

NAHUM 1:7 NIV

A Good Work Begun

*F*ather, Your Bible tells me You began a good work in me before I was born. All my life I've wanted to do right for You. Have You really kept Your hand on me all these years? What is Your plan for me?

I set into motion a fine masterpiece of you even before you were conceived. I still remember your first cry. Oh, what a sweet child you were—such a little one, made in My image. I recognized and loved your tender, caring heart from the time you were young. Through the years, I am guiding you in ways to accomplish My will. Each time you reach out to another and help, I rejoice.

You are the apple of My eye, My child. I love you with an everlasting love. You are My workmanship. I call you to serve Me. As you continue to love and obey Me, I am guiding you. Indeed, I have a purpose for your life.

Let my labor be fruitful through my faith in You, Father. Let my actions be prompted by the love You plant in my heart. Grant me endurance, inspired by the hope I have in You. Continue Your work in me, O God. In You I find fulfillment and purpose.

*And I am sure that God who
began the good work within you
will keep right on helping you grow
in his grace until his task within you is
finally finished on that day when
Jesus Christ returns.*

PHILIPPIANS 1:6 TLB

You Chose Me

I went to a shower today, Father. It was for an eight-year-old girl named Trisha. Her new parents are my friends. Several children came up for adoption at the same time for my friends to choose from. This doesn't happen very often.

They could have adopted a baby. But when they took one look at Trisha, the couple immediately fell in love with her. They're so excited to have her as their child, Father. They're already talking about the hopes and dreams they have for her as she grows up.

Is that how it was when You chose me? Did you see something special in me right from the beginning? Do You have hopes and dreams for me as I grow in You?

Not only did I choose you, dear child, but I wanted all of humankind to be My own and follow Me. Everyone has been called, but few choose to follow. I saw something special in you from the beginning. I treasured you before you were even interested in Me. You, My child, love Me because I first loved you. Walk, then, in My love; and see the wondrous hopes and dreams I have for you.

Thank You for choosing me, dear Father. I will follow You.

> *[Jesus said,] "You did not choose Me,*
> *but I chose you and appointed you*
> *that you should go and bear fruit,*
> *and that your fruit should remain."*
>
> JOHN 15:16 NKJV

You Are Mercy

A student in our classroom taught me a lesson of mercy and true forgiveness, Lord. She's a sweet, tenderhearted girl. When a boy in our room said mean things about her, she came to me in tears and complained. The three of us talked out the problem. I must admit I was frustrated with the boy's behavior. But she was different. When the boy was ready to ask forgiveness, she gave it in a second and accepted him again as her friend.

How much greater than this little girl's mercy is the kindness You show to me. I first experienced it when You forgave my sins and adopted me as Your own child. Even now in my struggles, You show Your constant compassion.

Sing of My mercy, dear one. Sing of My love forever. Let your friends and family know all about My faithfulness and forgiveness. My love for you stands firm and steadfast. When you err, I forgive you. When you are merciful, I grant you mercy. When you are loving, I shower you with love. When you are generous, I abundantly bless you. When you help the weak in their times of trouble, I am, in turn, always there to help you.

Thank You for Your mercy, Lord. Let me pass it on to others.

Instead, be kind to each other, tenderhearted,
forgiving one another,
just as God has forgiven you
because you belong to Christ.
EPHESIANS 4:32 TLB

I Love Your Ways

*T*he longer I know You, my Savior, the stronger my love for You grows. Your ways have become second nature to me. I think of Your Holy Spirit in my life, and I love everything about You more than ever. Your tenderness and steadiness give me assurance through each day.

When I carefully listen to Your direction and follow Your lead, I feel Your warm approval. When I become careless and open my mouth at the wrong times, I sense You silently cautioning me to stop what I'm doing and to change my attitude. I love You, dear Lord. I love Your being my best Friend, my Confidant, my Counselor, my Lord.

We walk this path of life together, dear child. It is called the way of holiness. It is only for those who willingly come with Me. Copy My deeds. Step in My footprints. Echo My words. Show My compassion. Hold tightly to My hand, lest you slip and lose your spiritual balance. Make My ways your ways. I shall faithfully lead you and never cause you to stray. I am the only Way, the Truth, and Life eternal. No one comes to My Father unless he or she is following Me.

I will place my feet in Your footprints, Lord. I will firmly hold Your hand.

Teach me to do Your will,
for You are my God; let Your good Spirit
lead me on level ground.

<small>PSALM 143:10 NASB</small>

Do You Pray for Me?

*L*ast week was discouraging, Lord. Nothing went right. I was driven to tears and wondered if You were even near. I didn't give up though. I brought my needs to You, asking for Your guidance. I could only share these troubles with You, Lord. No one else knew how I felt. Out of desperation, I took my hands off everything and asked You to intervene. Before long, I felt total peace. It was as though someone was praying for me. Still, no one else knew of my troubles.

Were You the One praying for me, Lord? Your Bible says Your Holy Spirit makes intercession for us according to God's will. When I had no more words with which to cry out for help and I gave my burdens to You, did You lift them from me anyway? Did You take them to my heavenly Father and plead my cause? This boggles my mind.

Yes, I prayed for you, My child. When you bring your concerns and cares to Me—your Lord—the Holy Spirit hears your prayers and intercedes on your behalf to the heavenly Father with groanings that cannot be uttered by anyone.

How grateful I am for Your praying for me, Lord.

In the same way the Spirit also helps our weakness;
for we do not know how to pray as we should,
but the Spirit Himself intercedes for us with groanings too deep for words;
and He who searches the hearts knows what the mind of the Spirit is,
because He intercedes for the saints according to the will of God.

ROMANS 8:26–27 NASB

I Will Follow You

*L*ord, I hear You talking to my heart to do something new for You. I'm really struggling with this. As You know, I don't handle change well. I like life planned out in one neatly wrapped package. I want to know what is going to happen from one day, one year to the next—even ten years down the road. But more than what I want, I must accept this calling You give me.

I can't get over how Simon Peter and Andrew dropped their nets without hesitation and went along with You when You said, "Come, follow Me." Grant me the same strength and faith You gave to them. Show me how to adhere to You without wavering.

I will follow You, my Lord. Reveal the great and mighty plans You have for me. Help me put my efforts wholeheartedly into Your service. Here with You, I look straight ahead. I will not long for the past.

Come, child. Dream My dreams. Catch the vision of the things I place before you to accomplish. See the spiritually hungry and how they need to know Me? The harvest of souls is plenty, but willing workers are few. In the same way the heavenly Father has commissioned Me, so am I sending you.

Yes, my Lord, I will follow You.

"Come, follow me," Jesus said,
"and I will send you out to fish for people."
MATTHEW 4:19 NIV

Will You Remain with Me?

*L*ord, I hear You calling me to serve You. This is a mountainous undertaking You have given to me. Everywhere I turn, I see the consequences of sin, pain, suffering, and uncertainty.

I don't have answers for these people with whom You call me to share Your love. What if I don't do things right? What if I break down under the load? I feel like Joshua just about to cross the Jordan River. Will You remain with me, no matter how difficult things get? Please stay close. Please go before me.

I, the Lord your God, will cross over ahead of you in this undertaking I am giving you, My dear one. Draw from My strength and courage, for your help comes from Me. Fear not. Be not terrified of the destruction caused by the evil one. Do not be discouraged. I am always with you. I am greater than anything you will confront. Be certain that no matter the circumstances, I will never abandon nor turn My back on you. As I once was with Moses and Joshua, so shall I now be with you.

Thank You for being my God. Thank You for holding tightly onto my hand and constantly reminding me not to fear. How grateful I am for Your being here with me. In You I trust and obey.

"Be strong! Be courageous!
Do not be afraid of them!
For the Lord your God will be with you.
He will neither fail you nor forsake you."

DEUTERONOMY 31:6 TLB

Popcorn Christian

I want to share You with everyone around me, dear Father. Sometimes I become fearful of saying the wrong things or being rejected, but I do much better now than I used to. When I was in elementary school, the opportunity would come to give testimonies of Your love in church. I longed to but felt as though glue held me to my seat.

When I grew old enough to be in the youth group, I would stand up, blurt out, "Jesus loves me," and sit down. Our youth leader had a perfect description of people like me. He called us popcorn Christians. He said we popped up, turned white, and sat down. My testimony wasn't too great; but it was the beginning of my learning to share.

The more I walk with You, Father, the more fantastic things I have to tell. Now I long to let others know of Your wonderful, life-giving love. Even still, there are times when I'm hesitant. That's when I take a deep breath and ask You if You want me to share. Much to my relief, You guide me. Your answer may be "yes"; "wait for the right time"; or "keep silent and pray."

Thank You for each time You lead and help me, through Your powerful holy presence, to tell others about You.

The Lord God has given me his words of wisdom
so that I may know what I should say to all these weary ones.
Morning by morning he wakens me
and opens my understanding to his will.

ISAIAH 50:4 TLB

Potpourri Presence

*L*ord Jesus, the heat of stress is coming at me from all sides. Difficult decisions need to be made quickly. There are insurmountable problems, pressures that are almost too much to bear, and endless bickering. Those around me who don't know You are looking to me as a Christian example. I'm turning to You right now, Lord, so all of this won't bring out the worst in me. Please help me, I pray.

I realize stress and anxiety aren't something new. You must have experienced a tremendous amount of strain while You were here on earth. The Bible tells how You were ridiculed, lied about, pressured, beaten, and finally crucified. I am awed at how You continued to love others, no matter who they were or what they did.

When You were crushed, Lord Jesus, You brought forth a pure Spirit, sweet as a rose. Fill and surround me with Your presence, Lord. Help me change this pressure into a Spirit-filled potpourri presence so others will recognize You in me and want to know You as their Savior.

Thank You, Lord, for helping us. Thank You, too, for the person who asked me later how I remained kind and calm. Speak to her heart while I tell her how it all comes from You.

So if you are suffering according to God's will,
keep on doing what is right
and trust yourself to the God who made you,
for he will never fail you.

1 PETER 4:19 TLB

I Want to Catch Your Vision

*L*ord God, I see people all around me suffering from sin's devastating blows. Some struggles are brought on by their own rebellious, uncaring actions. Others are suffering because they don't know You as their personal Savior—yet. But there are Christians who are grief-stricken by what sin is doing to those they love.

Surely You love each person far more than I am ever capable of doing, Lord. I want to catch Your vision. How can I reach these lost and struggling souls for You? I realize I will never be able to perceive all of this through Your eyes. If I did, I wouldn't be able to take it in. With my limited human comprehension, I struggle to acknowledge sad news reports and painful firsthand experiences and observations.

I'm only one person in this vast world. Please show me what I can do to help others accept You. Let me weep with them. Comfort them, I pray. Let me lead them to You. May Your Holy Spirit take over and bring them into Your loving arms. Help them accept You. Then I will celebrate with the angels. Let them be filled with joy, and I shall rejoice with them.

Thank You for a glimpse of Your vision, Lord God. I open my eyes and my heart to Your vision.

"I will pour out my Spirit upon all of you!
Your sons and daughters will prophesy; your old men will dream dreams,
and your young men see visions. And I will pour out my Spirit
even on your slaves, men and women alike."
JOEL 2:28–29 TLB

Seeds of Salvation

Thank You for giving me a portion of Your vision, Lord. I can see myself as Your servant scattering Your seeds of salvation everywhere I go. Fast. Slow. Steady. Constant. I'm actually planting Your upcoming Church! The Body of Christ. Like the dandelion seeds, some will germinate and grow; others will not.

In the same way flower seeds land on fertile soil, I pray those who hear about Your love and salvation will listen and accept You as their Savior. Remind me not to abandon them after they accept You but to nurture these souls with Your spiritual food and living water. Grant me faithfulness and time to pray with them, to search the verses in Your Bible together. In the process, let me grow along with those I care for.

Help me to believe in the ones I reach for You as they embark on their new walk with You, Lord. When they take their spiritual baby steps, stumble, and fall, grant me patience as You and I stoop down together and help them up, again and again.

I will never give up telling people about You. Even when they refuse or put off receiving You, I'll pray for them. Lord Jesus, I will keep scattering Your life-giving seeds of salvation to every available soul throughout the rest of my life.

[Jesus said,] "The farmer sows the word. . . .
[Some,] like seed sown on good soil,
hear the word, accept it, and produce a crop—
some thirty, some sixty, some a hundred times what was sown."
MARK 4:14, 20 NIV

Closing the Deal

*I*t's becoming a little easier to tell those I come in contact with each day about You, Lord. The more I'm around people, the more I hope and pray they recognize me as a Christian. Grant me opportunities to share Your love with them, I pray, and make me alert to the openings when they come.

The frightening part in leading someone to You is helping them take that final step of accepting You as their personal Savior. In a salesperson's words, it's the stage of "closing the deal."

Help me be keenly aware of this time when it comes, Lord. Remind me to take a deep breath, send up an arrow prayer for help from You, then invite this one to give his or her life to You. I'm so glad that this is when I can rely on You and allow Your Holy Spirit to step in, work, and change lives. I can lead people to You, but I am unable to save souls. Only You can do this, Lord.

Thank You for helping me lead each person to that final step of accepting You and for "closing the deal." I praise You for Your awesome power. Thank You for saving each precious one and making them Your own.

But as many as received him,
to them gave he power to become the sons of God,
even to them that believe on his name.

JOHN 1:12 KJV

I just watched the world news, Lord. New technology makes us seem closer together than ever before. Bad news: wars. Earthquakes. Tornadoes. Floods. Good news: people making peace. People helping people. New beginnings. Worldwide missions. Revivals. Sacrifices for others. Kindnesses shown. I treasure those good reports, Lord. When I hear bad news, I feel called to help however possible.

Lord, help when tragedy strikes. Be with leaders everywhere. Rally them to follow You. Watch over Your ministers, missionaries, and Christian workers. Grant each one protection, strength, wisdom, and plenty of love. Clothe them with Your holy armor. Let all people know Your love. Show me ways I can make a difference. Lord, I realize there are Christians all around the world who love and serve You. They are praying fervently for each other. Some pray for us! Thank You for them.

Help us as Your followers to join our prayers. Turn hearts to You. For those in bondage or free, You paid the price to truly free our souls. Help our hurting world call on You and obey Your will. Heal us. Restore us. Grant us the peace of heart that comes only from You.

[Jesus said,] "I am not praying for these alone but also for the future believers who will come to me because of the testimony of these. My prayer for all of them is that they will be of one heart and mind, just as you and I are, Father— that just as you are in me and I am in you, so they will be in us, and the world will believe you sent me."

JOHN 17:20–21 TLB

Why Me?

*I*f I could to see You face-to-face right now, Lord, I would have many questions to ask. When I try to answer them myself, I feel like I'm looking at everything through dark-colored glasses after coming in from the sunny outdoors. Nothing is very clear.

I can't see You, Lord, but Your presence is here with me. Assist me as You and I search the scriptures together. Please grant me insight, comfort, and assurance.

I want to know *why me?* Why was I one of the lucky ones to be saved when so many others are lost from You for eternity? The greatest day of my life was when I asked You into my heart and You became my Savior. You actually adopted me as Your child, Lord. How blessed and fortunate I feel.

Did I ask You to be my Savior first, or did You first knock at my heart's door? Did You choose me? What of the others? Your Bible says that You loved the entire world so much that anyone who believes in You will become Your own and will gain everlasting life.

My child, anyone who comes to Me with a humble, repentant heart shall be saved and become part of the kingdom of heaven.

Thank You, Lord, for calling us all.

[*Jesus said,*]
"*Whoever believes in Him should not perish
but have eternal life.*"
JOHN 3:15 NKJV

Do You Accept Me as Your Own?

I love You with all of my heart, soul, and mind, Father. I love You more than all else. I know You love me. But why do I not feel worthy of Your recognition? Do You really accept me as Your child? Is it because You created me, and I belong to You?

I cherish my children. I still remember their first cries. I fell in love with them while they were still in my womb. What a thrill when each little body stirred within me. And, oh, when I saw them! In my eyes, my babies were the most beautiful children in the world. I love them because they are mine, not because they had to earn my love.

Do You remember my first cry, Father? Do You perceive everything about me? Did You know and plan me before time—before I was even conceived? It was You who knit me in my mother's womb, wasn't it? Do You love and care for me just the way I am? Is it so, that I can trust in Your love and acceptance because You are my heavenly Father?

I love you, My child, with an everlasting love. You belong to Me.

How I praise and thank You. Though I'm undeserving of Your love, I can be sure I am Your own.

See how very much our heavenly Father loves us,
for he allows us to be called his children—
think of it—and we really are!

1 JOHN 3:1 TLB

Why Was I Born in These Times?

Everything is push button or flick of a switch these days, Lord. I enjoy the conveniences and technology we have at our fingertips. Yet I long for years gone by. While growing up, I heard stories of how "life was simpler back then." Lots of land. Nature everywhere to enjoy. Fewer restrictions. Certainly less traffic. I feel as though I've been placed in the wrong era. Why was I born during these times?

Do You have a purpose for my being here now? The Bible says You chose me when You planned creation, and my days are written in Your Book of Life. I'm amazed how You determined exactly when and where I would live.

You must have me placed here for a reason. In 2 Corinthians 6, You tell me now is the time You show me Your favor. Now is the time of my salvation—for me to worship and serve You. Thank You for giving me the right to choose. Because of Your love for me and mine for You, dear Lord, I choose to follow You anytime, anywhere. Thank You for promising me a future especially for me, filled with hope and joy.

I guess I'm not misplaced in time after all, Lord. In fact, I feel assured that You want me right where I am right now to glorify You.

For I know the plans I have for you, says the Lord.
They are plans for good and not for evil,
to give you a future and a hope.
In those days when you pray, I will listen.
JEREMIAH 29:11–12 TLB

Is My Life Significant to You?

*F*ather, all around me I see people accomplishing great things for You and humankind. Many folks are better looking, smarter, more educated, and wealthier than I am. The "wealthier" part doesn't bother me, but I feel limited in what I can do to serve You in other areas.

Is my life significant to You, Father? Does it matter to You that I struggle with these insecurities? Though I have little to give You, I love You and want to serve You with every part of my being. Perhaps I'm selling myself short. Increase my faith, I pray, and help me.

My dear one, take delight in the way I made you. For it is I who gave you your looks, your talents. You are My beautiful creation, brimming with gifts I love for you to share. I rejoice over you with singing. You are My child of great value, My treasured possession. I love to do good for you. I will inspire you as I plant you in this place, here and now, to serve Me.

Everything you say and do is important to Me, like ripples in a pond, affecting others around you. Trust Me. I am able to accomplish more with your life than you can ever imagine.

Thank You, Father. How worthy You are of my love and service.

May our Lord Jesus Christ himself and God our Father,
who loved us and by his grace gave us eternal encouragement and good hope,
encourage your hearts and strengthen you in every good deed and word.

2 Thessalonians 2:16–17 niv

Why Were We Given a Choice?

Lord, there are a lot of noble attitudes and actions coming from people in this world that bring happiness and peace. Others, however, are causing much pain and stress because of the indifference and hatred they demonstrate. If it saddens me, it must cause You tremendous pain. How can You stand us when we are so selfish and arrogant? Why were we given a choice of how we want to live?

Your love is greater than what I can comprehend. You look beyond our faults and see the possibilities of who we can become for You. Does my choosing to love and follow You mean more than if I were some kind of robot, ordered to do this or that? I think it does. Lord, forgive me when I falter and become self-centered or uncaring. Thank You for not giving up on me. Thank You for helping me to get back on course with You.

I wish sin would just go away. But as long as I'm forced to contend with it, I will. With all power given me from You, I shall do everything I can to make a difference. I love You, Lord. It is You I choose to live for.

"And if you be unwilling to serve the Lord,
choose this day whom you will serve. . .
but as for me and my house, we will serve the Lord."
JOSHUA 24:15 RSV

How Could You Leave Heaven for Me?

*B*efore You came here, Lord, You had everything. A throne. No sin, sadness, or pain. How could You leave heaven and Your Father's side to come to a world You knew would hate You? Why did You save me and make me Your child? I don't deserve it.

How sorry I am for causing You sorrow through my wasted years and actions before asking You into my life. No matter what good I do, I can never make it up. I love You, Lord. I'm grateful for Your love and forgiveness. You left heaven, knowing what would happen. Still, Your love for me and all humankind caused You to come. You left royalty to be born in a stable. You accepted ridicule and torture. And You died for me. Why, Lord?

You are My own, dear one. I came so you can know and rely on My love. I came here to overcome sin. Not because you deserve Me, but because I love you with an everlasting love. My desire is to lavish My love upon you and give you a life filled with inner peace and joy. Accept it. Treasure it, and live for Me.

Thank You, Lord, for leaving heaven and saving me. Your gracious love truly is sufficient. Let my soul magnify You in all I say and do.

And He said to me,
"My grace is sufficient for you,
for My strength is made perfect in weakness."
2 Corinthians 12:9 nkjv

How Do You Feel about Evil?

*M*any times, malicious, terrifying actions bring devastation beyond description. I run to You like a child, and I cry out, "Look, Father! See what they did?"

I hate the way wickedness tricks lost people. How do You feel about evil and wrongdoers? What about Your Son? Did You abandon Him when He bore my sins?

The Bible says to flee from evil. It declares that sin causes ruined lives and eternal death. I believe You despise evil, Father. But the people? You constantly plead for everyone to receive You.

I can't comprehend what happened when Your Son died. I do know Jesus took my sin and anguish upon His shoulders. Rejected by many, He paid the price. Your power provided escape from sin for all. You didn't interfere, Father. Still, You were there when the temple's veil tore from top to bottom, when the earth shook, the rocks split, and the tombs broke open and the dead came alive. You were there when the sick became well. You were there when the centurion exclaimed, *"Truly this was the Son of God!"* And You were there, Father, when Your Son victoriously rose from the grave!

Victories over wrongs still happen. Through them, You bring forth loving, caring people. Love conquers all. Truly You are my righteous Father. Truly Jesus *is* the Son of God!

Hold fast that which is good.
Abstain from all appearance of evil.
1 Thessalonians 5:21–22 kjv

Why Can't People Show More Love?

Lord, thank You for those in my life who love me. They give me joy. They make me laugh. They fill me with enthusiasm and pump life into me. But there is one who doesn't seem to have any love to give. No matter how hard I try to please or show kindness, this person shows little response. I usually go away feeling empty. How very sad. Not for me but for the one who lacks the ability to show love.

You must know other people who experience this, Lord. Do they have relatives or friends who put on such a stiff, rough exterior that no one can penetrate it with warmth and sincere thoughtfulness? What causes them to be so cold? When some are no longer alive, there is nothing we can do but leave it with You. Others are still here, however, never experiencing what real love is all about.

Please find a way to break through their uncaring veneer, I pray. No matter the cause, saturate and soften their calloused hearts with Your never-failing tenderness. Give them a glimpse of what real love is all about.

Remind me to pray each time I see the unlovable person I care about. Give them Your unfailing love through me.

Love never fails.
1 CORINTHIANS 13:8 NKJV

What Brings You Joy?

*Y*ou are my dearest Friend, Lord. I love taking walks with You and enjoying Your creation. I appreciate talking with You and sharing my joys, my concerns, and my secrets. When I'm upset, I come to You—my hiding place and my comfort. You are my refuge and strength. You help me with problems. I have no other friend like You, Lord.

I don't want to neglect our times together. When I do, emptiness grows inside me, and I miss out on Your direction. This must sadden You. Please keep me close. What brings You joy, Lord? Show me Your ways.

Come to Me once again, dear child. Give Me your worship and praise. Open your soul and share your life with Me. Oh, how I delight in you, when your days are filled with righteousness that shines like the dawn. I love it when the joy of your salvation glows like a blazing torch. Keep doing good, for this is My will. It pleases Me. Continue showing your love to Me and to others. As you do, My joy remains in you and your joy is made full in Me.

I praise You, O Lord. With all my might, I love You and want to share Your love with others. Teach me Your ways so the joy we share is made complete.

[Jesus said,]
"I have told you this so that my joy may be in you
and that your joy may be complete. My command is this:
Love each other as I have loved you."

JOHN 15:11–12 NIV

Are You Pleased with Me?

What will it be like when I meet You face-to-face, Lord? Some of my friends say they will stand in awe and praise You. But I feel unworthy. Will I be on my knees, with my head bent low? Do I deserve to appear before You?

Are You pleased with me? I love You with all my heart. Yet I have only a grain-sized faith. At times I mess up and get discouraged. Will I pass the tests of life? You are my rescuer, my only hope.

Your shortcomings are already forgiven, dear child. Your repentant heart causes Me to remember them no more. They are removed as far as the east is from the west. My grace has made you whole. You are cleansed and given a new life in My name. Once, your sins were like scarlet. Now you are made sparkling clean, as white as snow.

Keep loving Me, dear one, and obey My precepts. Seek Me first and My righteousness. Whenever you fail, I will help you start over. When you come before My throne, I will greet you with open arms. I will wipe away your tears and strife. I will lead you to My springs of living water, where you shall experience boundless joy forever.

Oh, what awesome grace I feel when You are pleased with me.

[Jesus said,]
*"But seek first the kingdom of God
and His righteousness."*
Matthew 6:33 nkjv

How Can You Use Me?

I want to be valuable to You, Lord. Every day, You shower Your blessings on me. How can You use me to glorify You? The Bible says Your first and greatest commandment is for me to love You with all my heart, soul, and mind. The second commandment is like it: to love my neighbor as much as I do myself. Is this the utmost way You can use me? By my showing love?

Some people are easy to love. But others are difficult to even like! Yet You say if I don't have Your love, my words and actions matter for nothing. I can't do this by my own strength. Please help me, Lord. Show me in Your Bible how to do this.

I also read how this love You want me to give is of You. It says when Your Spirit fills my life, You grant me a pure, unselfish love that puts off childish ways. Your love is patient and kind and doesn't demand its own way. During my daily frustrations, help me remember Your love isn't touchy or irritable. Help me not to hold grudges but to be willing to forgive. Teach me to look for the best in others and not be so quick to criticize.

Use me, Lord. Help me have a loving spirit in all I say and do.

Jesus replied:
"Love the Lord your God with all your heart
and with all your soul and with all your mind. . . .
Love your neighbor as yourself."
MATTHEW 22:37, 39 NIV

What Is Heaven Like?

*F*ather, I enjoy my life here on earth. I treasure my family, friends, and being able to worship You in church. And, oh, the blessings of camp meetings! It's like a little bit of heaven here on earth.

Thinking about heaven makes me homesick inside. Was my soul with You before I was born? What is heaven like? Will I really get to see You, Father? Will I know my loved ones who go there before me? Will my husband still be my husband? Or will we be one in Your body of Christ? Like Mary, may I sit at Your feet with no concern for time? I want to enjoy Your presence and praise You for eternity. I want to bring You my questions, and I will trust You to help me with each one.

Your Bible tells me I'll get to shed this earthly body. There will be no sin, sickness, or pain, no sadness or mourning. No longer will I need to fend off worry or strife. Best of all, I will see Your glorious Triune—God the Father, Son, and Holy Spirit. I will get to meet You face-to-face.

When I kneel before You in heaven, I imagine Your Son bending down, taking my hand, and saying, *"I paid the price for you to come here. Welcome home."*

"Behold. . .God Himself will be with them and be their God.
And God will wipe away every tear from their eyes;
there shall be no more death, nor sorrow, nor crying.
There shall be no more pain, for the former things have passed away."
REVELATION 21:3–4 NKJV

How Can I Help Others Know How Wonderful You Are?

*L*ord, I want others to realize how alive, wonderful, and personal You are. I try to explain it, but I often can't get the message across. How can I help them understand? Show me the way, Lord, so I can reach these people for You.

Mere words don't seem to be enough. How can people get to know You through me? Help me become a vibrant reflection of You. Let all I do and say be living proof of what pleases You. Help me to relax and simply allow You to use me however You wish. Anoint me with Your powerful Holy Spirit. Let me magnify Your name and show how marvelous and great You are. As I let my light shine out to the lives of others, I ask for Your Spirit to speak to their hearts. Whisper Your words of love to them.

Remind me to hold them up in prayer every day. Help me to commit each one of these souls to You and trust You to work in each of their hearts. Grant me patience to have confidence in Your timing. You know best how to reach them. Let me never give up on them and Your wondrous grace.

Thank You for revealing how glorious and awesome You are.

But this precious treasure—
this light and power that now shine within us—
is held in a perishable container, that is, in our weak bodies.
Everyone can see that the glorious power within
must be from God and is not our own.

2 Corinthians 4:7 tlb

How Can I Find Real Victory and Joy?

*L*ord, there are so many negative and discouraging things happening around and to me. I'm tired. My patience is worn thin. I'm discouraged because nothing seems to be going right. My hectic lifestyle has left me used up and exhausted.

Today, someone came up to me and asked how I was. My response was, "All right, under the circumstances." At that very moment, I felt You speaking to my heart. I was allowing myself to play a supportive role in the pessimistic attitude that causes me so much grief. Forgive me, Lord. How can I find real victory and joy in all circumstances?

I realize I've been focusing on everything that's wrong. Your Bible says You want me to think on whatever is honest, righteous, pure, good, upright, beneficial, and praiseworthy. When I'm tempted to become depressed, help me shove out the negative thoughts and meditate instead on You.

Thank You, Lord, for providing me the victory over bad habits in words or deeds. Help me not to tolerate any of them in my life. Thank You for letting me feast on Your scriptures. Cleanse my soul and fill me anew with Your holy presence. Thank You for granting me the victory and joy that come from You.

Now may the God of hope fill you with all joy and peace in believing, so that you will abound in hope by the power of the Holy Spirit.

ROMANS 15:13 NASB

My Example

$\mathcal{L}$ord Jesus, two little words I often hear You tell me are ringing in my ears: "Trust Me." It's easy to say I'm going to trust You. When I'm pressed to put my words into action, it's a whole different story. Trust? Be confident? Rely? Wait? This is difficult for me.

I'm a doer, Lord. This isn't always good, especially when I should be waiting on You. I want everything done yesterday—microwave style. If I could do things instantly, I would be all for doing so. Relying on You shouldn't be impossible. When I lack trust, I'm not wholeheartedly submitting. I can't do this on my own, Lord. Help me, I pray. Teach me how to walk in Your footsteps.

Did You really want to come to this earth as a baby? You certainly didn't receive the comforts of a king. What about Your growing years, when others didn't understand how You felt, or Your preparing to die on the cross? You must have longed to be with Your Father. Still, He had a plan for You to fulfill, and You trusted in Him.

I'm only a Christian who wants to love and serve You. I'm not very strong on my own. I can only trust You through Your help and example. Please show me how.

Trust in the Lord God always,
for in the Lord Jehovah is your everlasting strength.
ISAIAH 26:4 TLB

Guard of My Heart

Over and over I give You my pain and shortcomings. Each time I do, Father, You show me answers in Your Word of healing and assurance, of love and protection. I find myself often turning to Ephesians where it tells about Your spiritual armor and the way it helps me. First, I read about Your belt of truth. Then I learn about Your breastplate of righteousness.

I recall how the breastplate used by soldiers in Bible times was made of overlaid pieces, which didn't allow even the smallest weapon to penetrate. It protected the heart of the soldier. In the same way, I discover how Your breastplate of righteousness protects my heart from the harmful evil one. I know I have to keep listening to Your guidance and make sure I allow no careless cracks to form. I must stay close to You in order to get through the spiritual and emotional battles I face. I trust You to fight them on my behalf.

Somehow, step-by-step You help me realize I don't need to struggle with wrong. You are doing that for me. Your righteous Spirit cleanses and heals my hurts and eases my mind. Thank You, Father, for how You are the guardian of my heart, keeping me safely in Your care.

And the peace of God,
which surpasses all comprehension,
will guard your hearts and
your minds in Christ Jesus.
PHILIPPIANS 4:7 NASB

Your Blueprint

*F*ather, things seem off center in my life right now. I can't put my finger on it, but there's no harmony inside me. Like so many times before, I must back off from the needless distractions and take a good look at the things I need to learn of You. Teach me so my heart is right with Your will.

When You put my broken pieces back together years ago, Father, You began the rebuilding process in me. It was like You rolled out Your blueprint for my life and showed me what You wanted me to do—one step at a time, one day at a time. What a wonderful experience it was as I allowed You to go through every area of my existence and do some serious spiritual remodeling. The more You did, the more I saw things You wanted me to accomplish.

I sense that's what You are teaching me to do now. Show me through Your Word the designs You have for me. Pull me back to Your plan. Let me be the temple where You dwell. Fill me with Your peace and joy, satisfaction and love.

Thank You for giving me a blueprint to keep me on center with You.

For I know the plans I have for you, says the Lord.
They are plans for good and not for evil,
to give you a future and a hope.
JEREMIAH 29:11 TLB

Persevere with Promises

Thank You, dear Father, for never leaving me alone. No matter where I am or what circumstances I face, I'm confident You are with me—helping, guiding me every step of the way. Each time opposition comes, prompt me to face it without fear and trust You to work things out.

Some frustrating situations happen around me. But others occur within my heart. When I'm a part of the problem, help me be open to You and willing to change. Soften my stubborn will and make me pliable, I pray, so You can use me in whatever ways You see best. In doing this, I'm learning more how to trust You.

When answers don't come easily and problems aren't solved as quickly as I would like, I turn to Your Word for guidance and assurance from You. As I read Your promises, they seem to jump off the pages of my Bible like they were put there especially for me. Thank You for them, Father.

Grant me the presence of mind to recall and stand on the promises You give me. In so doing, You help keep my steps sure and right.

For God has said,
"I will never, never fail you nor forsake you."
HEBREWS 13:5 TLB

Beyond My Ability

*M*ore than anything, I am learning to trust You, Father. One of the pieces of spiritual armor I read about is Your shield of faith. It is all-encompassing. It has a way of covering and shielding me on every side.

I read in Bible history how some shields were made of wood, beveled like a large, shallow dishpan. The rim, often brass, held heavy thicknesses of hide in place. Soldiers frequently anointed the hide with oil, most likely to keep it from cracking. The oil made the shield slick so flaming arrows would glance off it. A soldier slipped his arm through the strap in back to hold it in place. He could swing it in any direction to protect all parts of his body.

Like fiery arrows in Bible times, I, too, am attacked by Satan's harmful ways, Father. I don't have the capacity to fight these things. I praise You for going beyond my ability during these spiritual battles. I believe You even help hold my shield of faith. Thank You for extinguishing the evil one's fiery darts, protecting me on every side. I'm so glad I can rely on Your power rather than my own. I put all my trust—all my faith—in You.

David shouted in reply, "You come to me with a sword and a spear, but I come to you in the name of the Lord of the armies of heaven and of Israel—the very God whom you have defied. Today the Lord will conquer you!"

1 SAMUEL 17:45–46 TLB

Working Circumstances for Good

I feel as though I'm waiting forever, Lord, for You to answer this prayer. I don't understand why it's taking so long. Forgive me for wanting my problems solved microwave style—here and now. Teach me to wait and be patient. Help me relax and leave everything in Your capable hands.

Thank You for helping me realize You have a far better picture of timing than I do. Now I put my faith in You and in the way You are handling things. You, dear Lord, know what is best and when it should be done.

You promise that everything works for good when I put my trust in You and Your purpose. I come to You in hope and faith, believing. You, dear Lord, are my comfort and shield. Because Your love rests upon me, my heart rejoices, and I trust completely in You.

As I bring this prayer to You, I don't know how things will work out. But You do. I thank and praise You for Your answers to come. I know You are already working on behalf of these concerns. You are my Lord, my God. All the circumstances, all the timing, I place in Your hands.

These troubles and sufferings of ours are, after all,
quite small and won't last very long.
Yet this short time of distress will result in
God's richest blessing upon us forever and ever!
2 Corinthians 4:17 TLB

Hope for the Future

*H*ow grateful I am for another piece of Your spiritual armor, Lord. It is Your helmet of salvation. By Your grace, I am saved from sin and hopelessness. Because of Your unfailing love for me and my love for You, I am and always will be Your child.

I read again how in Bible times soldiers wore helmets made of brass or thick leather that guarded their heads from deadly blows during battle. Thank You for the helmet of salvation You provide me that guards my thoughts and my soul.

Because of You, dear Lord, I have no worries for the future. I know You care for me as loving parents do their child. Because of You, I have hope for the future on this earth and a wonderful, eternal life to look forward to in heaven with You.

Thank You for guarding my thoughts and helping me focus on the things that are beneficial and constructive. Each day as I go about my activities, I pray You will give me a positive, healthy outlook. As You do, I will reflect Your ways to those around me.

Thank You, Lord, for Your hope. Thank You for Your helmet of salvation.

The LORD delights in those who fear him,
who put their hope in his unfailing love.
PSALM 147:11 NIV

The Battle Is Yours

*H*ow grateful I am that whatever situation I'm in, Lord, You are here with me. Thank You for going before me, standing behind and beside me, and covering me with Your protective presence.

When I face danger, You are my guardian. When I'm a victim of false accusations and gossip, You are my defender. When the tempter is hammering at my heart's door, You deflect his fiery darts. When I'm ill, You fight for me to regain my health. When my loved ones go through various trials, You, dear Lord, surround them with Your love and protection.

There are instances when I get anxious and would like to take things into my own hands. I impatiently want to solve the problems my way, in my timing. Please give me a firm warning to stop at this point and trust You.

The Bible says these conflicts I face aren't fought with swords or spears. They aren't against flesh and blood. They are between Your goodness and the spiritual forces of evil, the rulers of darkness. As I trust in You, my battles become Yours. I don't need to fight them or even worry about them. Thank You, Father, for loving and taking care of me and fighting my battles.

"Thus says the LORD to you,
'Fear not, and be not dismayed
at this great multitude;
for the battle is not yours but God's.'"
2 CHRONICLES 20:15 RSV

Making My Teaspoon a Shovel

Father, I've faced some huge mountains in my life. Some, through faith in You, I overcame. There was one, though, where no amount of faith I mustered or lengthy, pleading prayers I uttered made a bit of difference. That obtrusive mountain loomed before me, almost laughing in my face.

I was frightened and confused, Father. I wondered why I couldn't get it out of my life. I recall crying out to You through clenched teeth, "Why me, Lord?" I struggled, trying to move my mountain a teaspoonful at a time.

The challenges I faced tested my faith to the limit. Finally, I changed my plea to "Not my will, but Yours, Lord." That's when I handed my puny teaspoon over to You and stepped back. You knew a better way to move my mountain.

You taught me to trust You more and yield to whatever outcome You willed for me. My anxiety disappeared. My soul felt at peace. I watched in amazement while You worked. The mountain never moved, Father. What moved was my mountain of distrusting Your will. Thank You for how You made my little teaspoon into a hefty shovel. Before I knew it, You and I had tunneled through. In the process, You gave me wisdom more valuable than nuggets of gold.

*So Jesus said to them, "Because of your unbelief;
for assuredly, I say to you, if you have faith as a mustard seed,
you will say to this mountain, 'Move from here to there,'
and it will move; and nothing will be impossible for you."*
MATTHEW 17:20 NKJV

Behind It All

Thank You, dear Lord, for handling the hurt feelings, the heartbreak, the frightening events and temptations I'm forced to contend with every day of my life. Nothing is too difficult when I turn it over to You. Along with Your coming to my rescue when I ask, I realize there are times You spring into action before I know what's happening.

During these trials, one of my greatest temptations is to lash out at those who treat me unkindly—especially when I'm accused of something I didn't do. The test is to remain calm when I have done something with a good heart and am accused of having the wrong motives. These things really hurt, Lord. I feel the hair on the back of my neck rise with my self-righteous attitude. After all, those wrongs were supposed to be made right. That's when You get me to listen and help me realize I don't have to be "right" when I feel I'm right.

Thank You for reminding me that my anger shouldn't be focused at people who do wrong. Instead, I can be angry at sin and all the heartache it brings. Thank You for helping me to put this behind me so I can move forward in Your will.

For we are not fighting against people made of flesh and blood,
but against persons without bodies—the evil rulers of the unseen world,
those mighty satanic beings and great evil princes of darkness who rule this world;
and against huge numbers of wicked spirits in the spirit world.
So use every piece of God's armor to resist the enemy whenever he attacks,
and when it is all over, you will still be standing up.

Ephesians 6:12–13 TLB

In the Pits

*P*raise You, Father, for the way I can trust You when I'm in the pits. Not the pits of despair and discouragement, but the pits in the race I'm running for You. Each time I take a curve, I find You waiting for me, ready to fine-tune my life so I can be an effective Christian.

Here I am again, Father, ready for You to search my heart, my mind, my emotions, even my physical stamina. I wait patiently as You work within me, cleansing, taking apart and rebuilding things that need to be fixed. Unlike the races I've watched with my husband and boys, the tune-ups aren't quick with a pat on the back and I'm on my way. There is no set time with Your work. Several areas You are rebuilding in my life can be done quickly. Others, however, are slow and sometimes painful.

Cleanse me, Father. Remake and remold the broken areas in my life. Refuel me with Your Holy Spirit so I can run this race You place before me and come out victoriously in Your name.

I yield to You, Father. Here in the pits, I trust You and am confident in Your love as You tune me according to Your will.

Oh, how kind our Lord was,
for he showed me how to trust him and
become full of the love of Christ Jesus.
1 TIMOTHY 1:14 TLB

Stand Firm—Victoriously!

What incredible victories I experience, Lord, when I put on Your armor. Each time I do, I draw closer to You. As I draw closer to You, my trust in You grows. Thank You for leading me step-by-step and teaching me Your wise and certain truth and righteousness. Thank You for allowing me to experience Your wonderful peace. I praise You for assuring me of Your saving grace and the hope You give me for the future. The more I walk with You, the more my faith in You steadily grows. Thank You for Your Word and how its verses guide me through every hour of every day. Now, during this challenge I face, I depend on You again.

I praise You, Lord, for how You help me stand firm, fully trusting in You, no matter what the circumstance. Nothing is impossible when I depend on You to work things out in Your timing and in the way You know best. Thank You for the spiritual triumphs You give me. They come only from You. When victories happen, keep my mind free from self-pride. When I face possible defeat, let it not darken my heart. With You, dear Lord, there is no such thing as defeat. You see the whole picture. You are triumphant. You are the victor over all.

Therefore, take up the full armor of God,
so that you will be able to resist in the evil day,
and having done everything, to stand firm.

Ephesians 6:13 nasb

Privilege of Praise

What can I give You, O Lord, that You have not already given to me? You have provided me with life, salvation, and countless generous blessings. The only thing I can offer You in return is my praise. So here I am, lifting my hands and my heart to You in adoration and thanksgiving.

Thank You, dear Lord, for granting me the privilege of praising You. How grateful and humbled I am that You allow me to come into Your presence.

Thank You for welcoming me as Your own. To You, dear Lord, I bring glory and honor. I love to praise Your holy name. You are my Most High God. You are above everything else You have created. You are my very existence, the theme of my life. You cause my life to be fully complete. You cause me to have a beginning that is wrapped up in You. You cause my life to have no end. I find fulfillment in You, life everlasting and free from sin's grip.

How glorious, how wonderful You are, O Lord. I lift my praise to You all the time. With my every breath I revere You. My soul rejoices in You. With my whole being, with all my might, I exalt Your holy name.

Bless the LORD, O my soul: and all that is within me,
bless his holy name. Bless the LORD,
O my soul, and forget not all his benefits.
PSALM 103:1–2 KJV

Sing Praises

*H*ere I am, Lord, at Your footstool, lifting my heart in songs of praise and thanksgiving. Day in and day out, no matter what time it is or where I am, I sing to You my adulation.

How good it is to glorify Your holy name! How delightful it is to acknowledge You in Your sacred presence. I sing out my thanks to You, O Lord God. Here I give You my all.

How marvelous You are. When I think of the wonders You have shown me, I cannot count them all. Because of who You are, my soul fills with gladness. I sing praises to You, the Most High.

Although I'm alone right now and my voice holds little talent, I want my praises to sound like a grand choir, with harps and violins and drums and cymbals. See my heart, my love for You, O Lord? Take delight, I pray, in my sacrifice of praise.

I pay tribute to You. From my rising in the morning, to my working through the day, to my resting at night, I sing praises. Some songs may be at the top of my voice. Others, I hum continually in my heart and mind. To You, Lord God, I sing praise.

Oh, sing to the LORD a new song!
Sing to the LORD, all the earth.
Sing to the LORD, bless His name.
PSALM 96:1–2 NKJV

Your Word

Thank You, Father God, for Your sure, true Word—Your Bible. When I read Your words and apply them to my heart and mind, I have complete confidence in You. Fears and doubts shatter, exposing the real truths—truths of Your love and faithfulness.

It is You I believe and trust. It is You who safely guards me. Everything I have, all my goals and dreams, I commit to You. My past, my present, and my future are in Your hands. I praise You that through the promises of Your Word, nothing can ever separate me from Your love. During good or fearful times, whether I'm here at home or far away overseas, You are with me every single minute.

Thank You for guiding me each day through Your Word. Thank You that I can tuck away Your lessons in my mind. When I'm confronted with temptations and trials, all I need to do is remember one of Your promises, and the devil flees. Your decrees are my greatest weapon against wrong. They are sharper than a two-edged sword.

How I praise You, Father God, for using Your Word to teach me. Thank You for anointing Your Word with Your Spirit for comforting and encouraging me as I walk with You.

For the word of the LORD is right and true;
he is faithful in all he does.
PSALM 33:4 NIV

153

For Carrying Me

*W*hen the things of this world crushed in and caused me to crumble, You carried me, Father. When I poured out my troubles to others and could find no one to really understand, You carried me. When I faltered and lost my way and struggled to put one foot in front of the other, You were the One who carried me.

Now I know not to lean on my own abilities. Although my friends and loved ones are dear, You are the One I can completely depend upon. I no longer try to be strong, for my strength lies in You. Thank You, dear Lord, for stooping down, picking me up in Your loving arms, and carrying me.

Thank You for helping me never to give up. No matter the circumstances, I praise You for being with me and showing me the way. When I'm unable to see around the next bend and wonder if there really is light at the end of the tunnel, Your light leads the way. I praise You, Father, for still carrying me.

Someday these troubles and trials will be over. I look forward to the day when You carry me once more to be with You in heaven. In the meantime, Father, I'll keep trusting, serving, and leaning on You.

[God said,] "I am with you;
that is all you need.
My power shows up best in weak people."
2 CORINTHIANS 12:9 TLB

Praise You for Hope

I praise You, O Lord, for giving me hope. When I was lost and had no way to turn, You saved me. You turned my life around and gave me a positive anticipation for the future. You gave me hope not only for the future here on this earth, but for the future into eternity.

I seek Your wise guidance, Lord. Let my mouth praise You. Let me honor You with everything I do. Through You I experience a spiritually rich life filled with enthusiasm and joy. As I synchronize my walk with Yours, I know I can't lose. You, dear Lord, are my desire, my existence, my entire being.

Some say You don't care about Your children. But I know that isn't true. You cause Your favor and love to shine upon me—not only upon me, but on all who love and serve You.

I praise You for being my tower of refuge, my place of safety when things go wrong. How grateful I am for the way You bring me through countless challenges and bless me beyond measure. You have a way of weaving Your blessing of calm assurance in and out of everything in my life. Hope in You proved true yesterday. Hope in You still abides today. And Your certain hope shall remain tomorrow.

Thank You, Lord. How I praise Your name!

May your unfailing love be with us, LORD,
even as we put our hope in you.
PSALM 33:22 NIV

Your Holy Ways

Holy are Your ways, Lord Jesus. Pure and faultless You are! Nothing in heaven or on earth can compare to You. No one can measure up to Your purity. The sun, the moon, and the stars are only inanimate objects and a part of Your creation. They can't begin to compare to You. What of humankind with our faults and frailties? In no way do we measure up to Your hallowed righteousness.

You set a perfect example when You lived here on earth. You were tempted. You were misunderstood and mistreated. You faced stress far greater than I can imagine. You were bruised and afflicted. Through all of this, Jesus, You never wavered in Your purity and obedience to Your Father. You were true and faithful, even during Your last moments on the cross.

How can I be holy, Lord? My heart longs to be like You. Lead me along the right paths, I pray. Share Your holiness with me. Fill and surround me with Your sweet presence. Teach me to walk in the footprints of Your righteousness, dear Lord. Let my heart be united with Yours. Grant me the power to overcome evil with good and reflect Your holy ways.

Teach me Your way, O LORD; I will walk in Your truth;
unite my heart to fear Your name. I will give thanks to You,
O Lord my God, with all my heart,
and will glorify Your name forever.
PSALM 86:11–12 NASB

A Sweet Fragrance

*L*ord God, I come to You with my heart and hands lifted in praise to Your holy name. Hear me as I call to You. Guard my mind, my intent, and my mouth as I come to You in prayer. May the words of my mouth and the most inner parts of my heart bring praises as a pure, sweet fragrance to You, O God.

I want to glorify Your name throughout my day, from the rising of the sun in the morning to its setting at day's end. When I awaken, You hear my praises. I sense Your glorious presence. I ask that every word I speak be lifted to You. Oh, I praise You with all my being. You feed and satisfy my soul all day long.

When my head sinks to my pillow at night, I think of You. I lift sweet fragrances of praise and thanksgiving to You again for Your wondrous help and guidance. Uplifting songs of adoration flow through my mind. I nestle in the shadow of Your wings. My soul clings to You while You hold me with Your right hand. I fall asleep, knowing Your warm comfort and protection. How dear, how sweet You are, my God.

My voice You shall hear in the morning, O LORD. . . .
Let my prayer be set before You as incense,
the lifting up of my hands as the evening sacrifice.
PSALMS 5:3; 141:2 NKJV

My Heritage

How can I comprehend Your adopting me as Your child, Father? There is no way. Still, I can completely trust You and the promises in Your Bible. Thank You for giving me Your marvelous heritage—one filled with peace of heart, deep inner joy, and a certain hope for the future You have planned for me.

Praise You for being my beloved Father and giving me Your Son, Jesus. You are my all in all. You are the strength of my heart. In You I have a fulfilling life here on earth and eternal life awaiting me with You in heaven.

Thank You for safely guarding everything I give You until the day of Your return. You love and care for me like a devoted parent. No matter where I am, I'm grateful You are only a prayer away. Thank You for being more than near. Thank You for living within my heart.

I'm grateful that I can place my identity in You. I've taken on the name of Your Son, Jesus Christ. I'm a follower of Christ. Yes, Father, thanks to You, I'm a Christian. I count it a privilege of being Your child—a child of the King of kings! Thank You for giving me the greatest heritage ever, a heritage in You.

*Yet to all who received him, to those who believed
in his name, he gave the right to become children of God—
children born not of natural descent,
nor of human decision or a husband's will,
but born of God.*

JOHN 1:12–13 NIV

Your Assurance

When I gave my heart to You, Lord, You established a never-ending covenant with me. You promised to be with me all the days of my life and into eternity. That step of faith I took—choosing life with You over spiritual death and destruction—released Your power to make me pure in the sight of God, my Father.

I praise You, O Lord, for the assurance that You are my Lord and my Savior. Because of Your loving assurance, I know in whom I believe. I'm convinced, without a doubt, that You are totally able to keep everything I commit to You. Everything I place in Your hands is safely guarded and protected by Your unfailing love.

Thank You for Your abiding presence day and night. Praise You for Your promise that You will never leave me or abandon me.

No one or no thing can keep Your love from me. Absolutely nothing has enough power to separate me from Your love. Not hardship or famine, not sickness or danger. Neither will life nor death. Evil cannot. Certainly the angels will not. Nor will the past, the present, or the future. Thank You, my Lord, for Your constant assurance and abiding love. Thank You for being with me all the days of my life.

For I know whom I have believed
and am persuaded that He is able to keep
what I have committed to Him until that Day.

2 TIMOTHY 1:12 NKJV

Stepping-Stones of Courage

*W*hen I read in the book of Genesis about the way Joseph's brothers threw him into a deadly pit, I thought of how frightened he must have been. I'm thankful for Your helping him and giving him courage. Although Joseph was pulled from the pit, it didn't solve his problems. You helped and guided him during the following difficult years. Thank You for being with him and for his faithfulness to You. No one had the power to break Joseph.

During his years in bondage, You gave him countless blessings. When he was falsely accused, You gave him honor. You helped him step over the stones of cruelty and stand firmly on a foundation of compassion and love.

When I was in the pit of despair, Lord, I felt like I was being buried under trials. Like huge rocks, my troubles piled up around me. Hurts and hopelessness were breaking my heart. The only way I could see was up. When I looked up, You were there.

I praise You for showing me how to take those terrible boulders and change them into stepping-stones toward victory. Each time I took a step, I could sense Your holding my hand, steadying me and giving me courage.

Thank You, Lord, for providing me stepping-stones of courage so I could experience numerous victories in You!

The steps of a good man are ordered by the LORD,
and He delights in his way.
PSALM 37:23 NKJV

Abundant Life

*B*ecause You are my Lord, my life is filled with joy and fulfillment. How blessed I am for putting my trust in You. To You, O Lord, I lift my praise with all my heart. In all my ways, I want to bless Your holy name.

Thank You for choosing me to become Your child. I praise You for looking for the best in me, for giving me certain talents. Thank You for handpicking what You want for me and helping me realize ways I can serve You. Praise You, Lord, for filling my life with purpose. Because of Your love for me, I have a reason to be here—a reason to love and serve You with all my strength and might.

I don't want to waste my life making material things my first love. Instead, I want to spend my life loving and trusting You. In You, Lord, I grow and thrive and have my motivation for living. It's an exciting life that's driven by Your divine will. It's a life of joy, everlasting and free from sin.

I praise You for the glorious plans You have for me. Your plans fill me with anticipation and hope. Thank You for putting me here to serve You, now and forever. Praise You, Lord, for coming to this earth and giving me abundant life.

[Jesus said,] "I have come that they may have life,
and that they may have it more abundantly."
JOHN 10:10 NKJV

161

Restoration

*M*y soul offers praise to You, O God, for how many times You have wrapped Your healing arms around me and restored me to wellness. I can't count the number of days of illness, heartbreak, and mental and emotional despair I've experienced. I occasionally wondered if there was any way back to recovery. Some sicknesses were so overwhelming I couldn't see the light at the end of the tunnel—only impossibilities. Yet deep within my heart, I knew all things were possible when I turned my needs for restoration over to You to work out in Your own way.

Several struggles with illness were severe enough to where I couldn't let them go. Whenever this happened, You helped me realize I was claiming sickness as a part of me.

Little by little, You taught me how to let it go and quit nursing my injured being. When I learned to allow You as my Great Physician to take these things away and renew me, I was on my way toward being healed.

Thank You for comforting me. Because of Your love, You bound up my brokenness and gave me strength to overcome all that I went through. I praise You for the way You took my damaged body, mind, and spirit and restored me to wholeness in You.

He heals the brokenhearted
and binds up their wounds.
PSALM 147:3 NIV

Making Life Count

J praise You, Lord, for showing me I'm not here by chance. I'm here because You want me, and I really matter to You. Thank You for making my life count. You give me direction and purpose. You help me visualize Your reasons for putting me here. You provide me with dreams for my future—a future in which Your will and mine are carefully knit together as one.

It doesn't matter whether I'm eight years old, eighteen, or eighty. Through the stages of my life, You call me to do special things for You. What an adventure it is—going through each day together!

The things You accomplish go far beyond my imagination. Through Your life-giving power working within me, little things I do will ripple out to others and down through generations. What You accomplish through me affects lives for eternity.

Someday when age causes me to slow down, I pray for You to help me look beyond bitterness and disappointments and think on how You have made my life count. Let me always see the big picture of Your purpose and savor memories of dear ones brought into Your family. Keep my mind and heart steadfastly fixed on You, my eternal Rock. In all circumstances I trust in You, Lord. Thank You for giving me a life that really counts.

The LORD will accomplish what concerns me;
Your lovingkindness, O LORD, is everlasting.

PSALM 138:8 NASB

Victory in You

Thank You for the hope and confidence You place within me, Lord. Thank You for helping me shed the life of being a victim. You are the One who makes me a victor. Because I trust in You, I gain Your wisdom to make right decisions that are within Your will and are best for me.

I praise You that I need not worry about anything. Instead, I pray about what comes my way and seek Your direction. I trust You, Lord, to work things out for the best.

I praise You for helping me with daily decisions. When I'm confused and don't know how to pray, You are near, beseeching Your Father for me. Oh, You understand me so well.

As I seek Your will and walk in Your ways, I'm grateful that You go with me and give me triumph. Thank You for helping me to be stalwart and courageous in times of difficulty. With You by my side, I can overcome fear, trusting You to banish it. Should it return, I know You will remove it again.

This victorious life doesn't come from weak efforts on my part. Instead, I praise You for being the conqueror over wrong and for providing me with victory.

[Jesus said,] "I have told you these things,
so that in me you may have peace.
In this world you will have trouble.
But take heart! I have overcome the world."

JOHN 16:33 NIV

The Beginning and the End

*I*f You were to roll out the scroll of time before me—the past, the present, the future, eternity—I wouldn't be able to take it in. If You showed me the secrets You revealed to John about heaven and time without end, I still could not comprehend them. How measureless, how everlasting You are, O God.

I bow down and worship You, the Alpha and the Omega, the Beginning and the End. You were, before all else began. You were in the beginning, You are with me now, and forever You shall be. You, O God, are the primary cause of everything. You are head over all, in and through all.

You set up the heavens and shaped the great rivers and the deep parts of the seas. You established the confines of the waters, instructing them to remain within their boundaries.

I worship You, O God, O Three in One. You were here as my Father, forming the plan for my life. Born a baby, You sacrificed Yourself for my sins. You became my Savior and my King. You are here as my Comforter, always with me.

O God, Alpha and Omega, the Beginning and the End, how I worship You.

"I am the Alpha and the Omega,
the Beginning and the End," says the Lord,
"who is and who was and who is to come, the Almighty."

REVELATION 1:8 NKJV

The Word

I bring honor to You, my God. You are Logos, the Word. You are the very existence of wisdom and power. Through the Word, I am learning to understand how wonderful and marvelous You are. Through the powerful Word, You came into my life and changed me.

Even before the world was, the Word was with God. You, the Word, are God. Through You, life was given. You are the light of life that shines brightly into the darkest corners.

In Your mighty wisdom and power, You embarked on a course driven with purpose, down through the ages, to come to earth.

How grateful I am for the way You humbled Yourself and became a little human baby, born of a virgin, cradled in a straw-filled manger. It is through this that humankind was able to see Your glory. You are the magnificent one and only God, who came from the Father, filled with truth and grace.

How can such a thing be possible? I only know it is true, because the Bible says so and You live within my heart. Thank You for providing me with a new life in You.

Glory be to You, God, the living Word who dwells among us.

In the beginning was the Word,
and the Word was with God,
and the Word was God.
He was in the beginning with God.

JOHN 1:1–2 NASB

Strong Creator

*G*lory, laud, and honor I bring to You, my strong Creator, for You made the heavens, the earth, the oceans, and all that is in them. So marvelous is Your craftsmanship, even creation itself tells of Your magnificence. You spoke a righteous command, and outer space was fashioned. Countless stars fell into place at Your command. You made the waters and caused them to pour into immense rivers and lakes. You spoke again and set the world into motion.

I look at this vast creation and how glorious it is. It's nothing compared to You, the Lord of all creation. What of humankind? We are only a fleck of dust. You pick up a desert island like a feather and reposition it from one place to another. You restrain the oceans with Your capable hands. You measure the universe. You weigh the mountains.

Every time I look into the darkened skies and see the work of Your fingers, I'm filled with wonder. I am amazed at how You made the moon and countless stars. I'm dumbfounded by Your love and care for a mere person like me.

I praise and honor You, God, for creating all of this, and for creating me.

When I consider Your heavens, the work of Your fingers,
the moon and the stars, which You have ordained,
what is man that You are mindful of him,
and the son of man that You visit him?

PSALM 8:3–4 NKJV

Righteous God

ere, I come before You on bended knee, O righteous God. Holy, holy, holy are You, God Almighty. How pure and honorable You are. Your presence surrounds me to the point I feel I'm on holy ground and should remove my shoes. Every day I see Your just dealings as You help me make right choices. You fill my heart with security and love because I can completely depend on Your holiness. Even the heavens can't compare to Your devout ways. There is no one like You, Most Holy God.

Who else do I have in heaven but You? No one matters more to me. You are the certainty I can look to, O God. When I'm faced with temptation, You provide the power I need to live victoriously. When I stand before You, the deeds I consider righteous will be only like filthy rags, for I am not just and good on my own. You washed everything in my life and made me clean. Because of Your love for me, You have forgiven my sins and clothed me with the attire of Your salvation. You have draped Your cloak of righteousness over my shoulders.

I praise and thank You for being my righteous God forever and forever.

"And there is no God apart from me,
a righteous God and a Savior;
there is none but me."
Isaiah 45:21 niv

Daddy

The time has finally come when I have a chance to talk with You, my Lord. I steal away to my quiet spot to worship You with my love and praise. Your tender presence surrounds me like a warm, comforting blanket. You're not far away on some pedestal. You are here with me, right now.

I worship You, my Abba Father. Abba means "Daddy." How true it is. You are my heavenly Daddy. You are like a caring father; I can talk with You for hours, and You never tire of listening. You are tender and sympathetic each time I come to You in prayer.

Your loving care for me is endless. Your watchfulness begins anew each day. I will never forget the mercy and grace You bestow upon me. You give me food. You always keep Your promises. When I start to waver, You remain near and keep me from stumbling. You watch over me all night long while I sleep. You spread Your wings over me like an eagle does over her young. You know me so well—inside and out. You understand my strengths and weaknesses, my concerns, my wants and dreams.

I lift my hands in praise and give tribute to You, my dear Daddy God. Thank You for loving and caring for me.

For you did not receive the spirit of bondage again to fear,
but you received the Spirit of adoption
by whom we cry out, "Abba, Father."
ROMANS 8:15 NKJV

Merciful and Gracious God

I come before You filled with adoration, Jehovah Elohim, my merciful God. I can only begin to thank You for Your kindness and mercy. You are gentle, patient, slow to become angry. The love You show to every person lasts beyond any measure of time. Amazingly, no matter if we deserve it or not, You keep loving us and desperately want all of us to know You as Savior and Lord.

Thank You for forgiving my sins and demonstrating Your steadfast love. Because of Your tenderhearted compassion, I am grateful to You and will honor You in every area of my life.

I offer my thanks to You, my God, for Your goodness, for Your mercy and graciousness that will remain with me forever. I give You my will, because You have given me a new life, and Your mercy and graciousness remain with me forever. I will follow You all the days of my life because of the mighty wonders You show me. In all things, I will trust You and not be afraid, because You keep and protect me with Your outstretched arms.

How I adore You, my Jehovah Elohim, my merciful, gracious God!

"Praise the LORD of hosts,
for the LORD is good,
for His mercy endures forever."
JEREMIAH 33:11 NKJV

Provider

My God, my Provider, I hold You in highest regard for all You do to care for me. I bring my needs to You and trust You with them. No matter what I face, it's never too difficult for You to handle.

I am so glad to be Your child. You provide for me. You have an amazing way of knowing what I require even before I do! I possess nothing in myself. In You, Jehovah Jireh, I benefit from everything. In light of the miracles I have experienced during my walk with You, I lift my heart in worship. My help truly does come from You.

You are constantly watching over me. In famine You feed me. In sickness You restore my strength. Somehow You supply my needs. Your blessings come directly from Your riches in heaven to me, Your child. Thank You for Your promise that You will never leave me nor forsake me. When I consider the way You are the strength of my life and how You shield me from danger, I am filled with gratitude. I trust in You, and You help me. As a result of Your love, a new joy bubbles within my soul.

Thank You for being Jehovah Jireh, my Provider.

Blessed are those whose help is the God of Jacob,
whose hope is in the Lord their God.

PSALM 146:5 NIV

Wonderful

*H*ow can I thank You enough for being my wonderful Lord? Deep gratitude fills me when I think of how You set salvation's plan into motion before time began. You knew we would fall into hopeless, sinful lifestyles. Sadness, self destruction, and despair resulted from evil's snare. Yet You still loved us and followed through with Your plan. Prophets, kings, and great leaders came and went through the ages. Then You came to earth and dwelt among us.

What a wonderful way You stepped from eternity into time. You were born of a virgin, took on humility and self denial, and became one of us. Only then could we better understand and follow Your example. You became our Teacher and Savior. You conquered evil by dying, rising from the grave, and ascending into heaven. What wonderful love You showed by sacrificing Yourself for this world. Your holy and righteous ways caused You to stand alone, shatter sin's hold, and free humankind from despair.

You, dear God, are separate, distinguished; greater than anyone else. You are exalted above creation. You are magnificent! Your glory goes beyond compare. I can't begin to imagine Your infinite power.

I worship You. I love and adore You, my wonderful Lord.

And His name will be called Wonderful.
ISAIAH 9:6 NASB

Counselor

*O*nce again I come to You, and we work through tough problems together. Here at Your feet I seek Your guidance and find wise answers. Thank You for being my Counselor, my Guide. Your words are filled with wisdom. You give me good advice and common sense. Your teaching lights the course ahead of me. As I heed Your instructions and obey, You keep me from stumbling.

How wise and all-knowing You are, my God. Without Your help, I don't always make right choices. You perceive things far beyond my abilities, and I trust You to guide me in everything I say and do. It's becoming easier to put You first. I experience Your peace and joy. Each time I listen and obey, I thank You for crowning my efforts with success.

I don't have the insight to plan what course in life I should take. When I become anxious and get ahead of You, I praise You for whispering to me, "Go this way. Follow where I lead." I worship You, my God, my Counselor. I commit my endeavors to You. I honor and trust You, even when I don't understand why things are happening the way they are.

Thank You for guiding me through my whole life. Thank You for being my Counselor.

[Jesus said,] "And I will ask the Father,
and he will give you another advocate
to be with you forever—the Spirit of truth."
JOHN 14:16–17 NIV

Mighty God

*P*raise and honor be to You, O Mighty God, for doing great and marvelous things for me. No one is as strong and powerful as You. You are awesome—filled with splendor and wonder. Your miracles have no boundaries. Your abilities are unlimited. Let everyone who comes into Your presence acknowledge Your greatness. Your magnitude goes beyond measure. You alone are holy. To You I bring glory and honor and praise.

Praise You, O Mighty God and Strong Warrior, for giving me victories each day. Thank You for Your mighty arms that reach out and protect me. You are in all and over all. As You march before me in Your greatness and strength, I shall not fear. Each day I place my confidence in You while You keep me safely in Your care.

Glory be to You, O God, for how Your almighty power works Your purpose for one such as I. How grateful I am that You do far greater things in my life than I ever envisioned. Your love and help go way ahead of my prayers, my needs, my thinking, or my expectations. To You I give glory forever.

Trials and heartaches happen. Wrongs appear to prevail. Yet through it all I know You, my Mighty God, are in charge. Praise You! You are the victor now and through eternity.

Great is our Lord, and mighty in power;
His understanding is infinite.
Psalm 147:5 nkjv

Everlasting Father

*H*ear my words of worship, O God, my Everlasting Father. You and You alone are my Father God. There is no other before You. You are everything to me. May all I say and think and do glorify You. Let me be joined to Your ways, that we may be one.

You are all-encompassing. You have always been here and forever shall be. I praise You for being my Father now and my Father of all time. Your years shall never cease.

Thank You for never changing. Circumstances and people change, but You remain steadfast and sure. Praise You, Everlasting Father, for being the same yesterday, today, and forever. I can depend on You and Your promises. Your Bible says You never go back on Your Word. You are trustworthy. You are Truth. Your love and compassion never end.

Praise You, Father, for Your unfailing love and kindness. You hide me in Your presence and snuggle me beneath Your strong hand—safe from sinful ways. I'm grateful for the way You store up blessings for me. Thank You for guiding me into the future. Your mercy passes on from one generation to the next, to those who trust and obey You.

O Everlasting Father, I worship You. O Everlasting Father, I give You my life, my all.

But the loving–kindness of the Lord is from
everlasting to everlasting to those who reverence him;
his salvation is to children's children of those
who are faithful to his covenant and remember to obey him!
PSALM 103:17–18 TLB

Prince of Peace

I lift my worship to You, O Prince of Peace. I praise You for the way You took my life of turmoil and strife and turned it around. You called me by name, and I followed You, instead of the selfish, uncertain things of this world. Thank You for cleansing my heart from wrongdoing and refilling it with boundless peace and contentment. Never has my life been fuller or happier. You, dear Lord, give me an inner calm that remains with me every day.

I praise You for Your just treatment, for shielding those who trust in You against heartless oppressors. How merciful and tender are Your ways. They are like heaven's sunrise breaking forth, bestowing light to those who struggle in darkness. Peace You offer every soul. It's a peace that comes only through You, the Messiah, the Lord of life. It's not a fragile peace like many seek from the world, but a tranquility of Spirit and common sense that comes only from You.

Thank You for a sound, permanent peace. It doesn't hinge upon circumstances, but fully depends upon Your lasting care. Thank You for giving an inner harmony far more wonderful than any human being can comprehend—one that keeps my thoughts and heart confident and at rest.

May You, O Prince of Peace, reign forever. Glory be to Your name!

*[Jesus said,] "And the peace I give isn't fragile
like the peace the world gives. So don't be troubled or afraid."*
JOHN 14:27 TLB

God with Us

Emmanuel. Dear Emmanuel, how I praise You for being with me every single day. You are so great. Even the heavens cannot contain You. Is there a way to measure Your love for humankind, when You left Your throne and came here to live among us? Thank You for Your loving forgiveness and truth, for becoming my Savior and Lord.

Thank You for Your promise that You will never abandon me nor disown me. You are my Helper. I will not be afraid, because I know You are protecting me wherever I go. Praise You for Your strength and steadfastness. No matter what comes my way, I know You boldly stand by my side, helping and guiding me.

When everything seems against me, You are here. Should others forsake me, You welcome and comfort me as Your own. I know You will always remain close to me during life's storms. You were here for me in the past, You are here for me now, and You shall be here for me beyond the end of time. You are the First and the Last. You are the One who died and the One who lives, now and forevermore.

I worship You, Emmanuel. I praise You for being near and abiding in my heart.

The Lord Almighty is with us;
the God of Jacob is our fortress.
Psalm 46:7 niv

Deliverer

I exalt You, Lord God, for You are my Deliverer. You found me running down a one-way path toward utter despair. When You called me, I cried out for You to rescue me. I could see no way out. But You did. You broke my shackles caused by sin, and You delivered me from a sad, aimless existence.

Thank You for rescuing me, dear Lord. Thank You for lowering Yourself and actually dying like a criminal on a cruel cross. Though You are God, You didn't command Your rights as God. You handed Yourself over as a ransom, and set me free.

How victorious is the way You were elevated to the loftiness of heaven and then sent to be my rescuer! How marvelous is the way You still show Your great love and bring good news to the anguished and afflicted. How excellent is the way You comfort the despairing, liberate hostages of sin, and open the spiritual eyes of those who seek You. How consoling is the way You reach out to those who mourn, wrap them in Your loving arms, and assure them of Your abiding love.

At the mere mention of Your name, I bow, proclaiming You my Deliverer.

"Offer to God thanksgiving,
and pay your vows to the Most High.
Call upon Me in the day of trouble;
I will deliver you,
and you shall glorify Me."
PSALM 50:14–15 NKJV

178

Solid Rock

Thank You, Lord God, for establishing my feet on Your solid, sure pathway rather than allowing me to stumble aimlessly on a foundation of shifting sand. You are my Lord, my mighty Rock, the basis for an unwavering life in You. You are the Messiah, the Son of the living God. My entire life is securely built on You, my Rock. The powers of hell can't even prevail against You.

You, mighty Rock, are the source of my salvation. There is no other who can save me from sin and wrong. I call on no one but You, the Son of the living God.

I am thankful that I can totally trust You, O Lord. Because of Your faithful love, I will allow no room in my life for mistrust. A mind unconvinced of Your faithfulness is as restless as debris on the ocean that is tossed to and fro by blustery weather.

I worship You, the One who loves me all the time. When anxiety or stress assails me, when scarcity of income strikes, when danger daunts, I will continue to trust in You.

When these things happen, I still find surety and victory in You. On You, my solid Rock, I shall always stand!

The Lord lives!
Blessed be my Rock!
Let the God of my salvation
be exalted.
PSALM 18:46 NKJV

Master and Teacher

I love sitting at Your feet, Lord, constantly learning new things from my Bible about You and Your wondrous ways. The more I study about You, the more I want to learn. It's like tapping into a life-giving, spiritual river of endless delight. The more I drink, the more I want to dive in and immerse myself in Your wise, sure resources for my life.

You, my Master and Teacher, are the certain truth that guides me to make right choices. What great and marvelous lessons You bring me from Your Father in heaven. When false leaders attempt to sway me toward careless ways, I measure what they say by Your sure, true Word. If it doesn't pass the test, I turn my back on such misguided teachings. Your Word is given by the inspiration of Your Father. Thank You, Lord, for how it straightens me out and helps me follow what is right. Thank You for preparing me for whatever comes my way. Your positive teachings bring sunshine to my soul.

You are so astounding, my Master and Teacher. I am grateful for Your farsighted wisdom. Forever teach me Your holy ways so I may walk in Your truth.

[Jesus said,] "You call Me Teacher and Lord,
and you say well, for so I am. . . .
For I have given you an example,
that you should do as I have done to you."
JOHN 13:13, 15 NKJV

Good Shepherd

I come before You in reverence and adulation, my God. I love You so much for being my Good Shepherd. I love the way You keep me near, leading me throughout each day. I love the way You whisper wise words to my heart and give me love and encouragement. Because I know You so well, I recognize Your voice when You speak to my heart.

Once You stood at my heart's door and constantly knocked, calling my name. I'm glad I finally opened that door and invited You into my life. You, O Lord, are my Good Shepherd. Thank You for providing me rest and strengthening my soul. Praise You for guiding me along the right way, like a shepherd guides his sheep. You use Your rod to lead me away from wrong, for I am Your name's sake. Your staff protects me from evil and harm. Thank You for filling my spiritual cup to overflowing with Your cleansing, healing oil.

When I face my final days of this earthly life, I know You will still be with me, and I shall have no fear. I will trust You, my Good Shepherd, to walk with me every step of the way through the valley leading from death to eternal life. I look forward, my Good Shepherd, to dwelling in heaven with You forever.

[Jesus said,] "I am the good shepherd;
I know my sheep and my sheep know me—
just as the Father knows me and I know the Father—
and I lay down my life for the sheep."
JOHN 10:14–15 NIV

Light of the World

O Lord, my Light in this dark world, how I adore You. You are the Light of my salvation, illuminating my way and directing me to a life of peace, hope, and joy. I no longer fear the darkness surrounding me. I trust in You and focus on Your presence. You keep my heart and mind in perfect peace. As I remain on Your lighted pathway, You make my feet sure on the treacherous curves. Thank You for leveling the uphill roads I'm forced to travel, for constantly smoothing out the bumps and potholes.

When bad news comes, I need not dread what lies ahead. Instead, I'm fully confident that You, my loving Lord, are taking care of my concerns every single day. You are the holy Light shining in my world. You are my refuge. No amount of darkness can hide Your glorious light.

I praise You for picking me up when I stumble and fall. Thank You for continually watching over me and caring for me, for being my defender. Thank You for protecting me day and night. Thank You for preserving my life and keeping me going in the right way.

Oh, how I worship and praise You. You are the wonderful Light of the World, the Light of my life.

Then Jesus spoke to them again, saying,
"I am the light of the world.
He [or she] who follows Me shall not walk in darkness,
but have the light of life."
JOHN 8:12 NKJV

Friend

You are dearer to me, Lord, than mere words can describe. I praise and adore You for being my Friend. I'm grateful for the way You love me all the time. What a comfort to know You are always with me and will never desert me. Thank You for loving me and looking for the best in me. Thank You for encouraging me as we walk through each day together. Thank You for listening to me and helping me with my daily decisions.

I can't imagine going through life without You as my Friend. I long for others in this world to experience the wonderful friendship You have to give. This friendship isn't limited just to me, but extends to everyone who willingly comes to You.

Lord, it's so good to know Your closeness and love. Everywhere, all the time, I feel Your warm presence surround me. The more we commune Friend with friend, the more You fill my thoughts and heart with Your love. The more I yield my will to You, the more my life is united with Yours. In all my ways, let me honor and glorify You. Let my actions and even my thoughts give You joy. I want my heart to be Your home.

How I love You, Lord, my most treasured Friend.

And now just as you trusted Christ to save you,
trust him, too, for each day's problems;
live in vital union with him.

Colossians 2:6 TLB

Messiah

I come before You, my Messiah, with a reverent heart. In humility I give You praise. You are the Anointed One—the One who delivers us from sin. Praise You, Prophet, Priest, and King. You are not an earthly prophet, not a priest or pastor of a church, not a political king or president of a nation, but our true Messiah—the Son of the living God.

You fulfilled the prophesies that foretold Your coming. You were born the Messiah, Jesus Christ the Savior. You grew in wisdom and stature from baby, to child, to the Son of Man. You were baptized and tempted. You overcame temptation. You became a servant, filled with humility and compassion. When You suffered and died on the cross, You were the very power and wisdom of God. My soul wells with gratitude for how You also became my Savior.

You, the divinely appointed King, bring God's salvation plan to all who are willing to receive You. Your followers are known as Christians—those who belong to Christ now and forever.

Thank You for bringing victory over sin. You don't bring this victory through physical force or violence, but through Your love, humility, and kindness. Truly the Father has anointed You with the oil of joy and gladness.

I bring honor and praise to You, my Messiah, my Lord!

The woman said to Him,
"I know that Messiah is coming (He who is called Christ);
when that One comes, He will declare all things to us."
Jesus said to her, "I who speak to you am He."
JOHN 4:25–26 NASB

Lord of Hosts

*G*lory be to You, O God, my Lord of Hosts. You are Creator and Ruler of everything: the heavens, the earth, and the entirety of that which exists through time and space. You made it all and are Ruler over it all. The stars, the moon, and the galaxies were created by You. Although these things are lovely, they aren't made for us to worship. Only You are my Lord God. Although angels and heavenly hosts reflect Your glorious miracles and handiwork, You did not create them for us to pray to or to consider divine. You reign over the angels as well.

When spiritual or physical battles are fought, You are the Mighty God of warriors. When victories are won, You are in charge. You are strong and mighty in battle. You are the Lord of Hosts, the King of Glory. Through turmoil, uncertainty, and despair, You are my refuge and strength. How blessed I am, trusting and obeying You. You are the Most High God.

In my quiet place, I worship You. In Your church sanctuary, I love bowing before You. I adore You, my Lord God. Praise I bring to You. Reverence and honor I lift to You! I look forward with longing to worshiping You, Lord of Hosts, when I someday meet You in heaven.

"Holy, holy, holy is the LORD of hosts;
the whole earth is full of His glory!"
ISAIAH 6:3 NKJV

Comforter and Helper

I come into Your presence, my Comforter and Helper, to worship and praise You. Thank You for being with me all the time. I love the way You speak to me deep within my heart and tell me I really do belong to You. Thank You for giving me confidence. I need not cringe or be fearful of troubles surrounding me, for You are always with me.

Truly You are my Sustainer, the One who keeps me going when I become weary. When spiritual battles rage, You rescue me. When I face daily problems, You help me. Thank You for teaching me how to pray when I can't express how I feel. Thank You for giving me hope and joy and Your power. Because of Your abiding presence, I can hold my head up with surety and confidence. No matter what happens, I trust in You. All is well, for I am in Your care.

You are so dear to me, my Comforter. I enjoy Your friendship all the time. I take pleasure in sharing good happenings with You. I'm grateful for Your reassuring love and help when I face trouble. When I feel alone, You are my Advocate. Thank You for encouraging me and cheering me on.

I worship You, my Comforter, my Helper. My words of praise can't begin to describe Your loving-kindness.

[Jesus said,] And I will pray the Father,
and he shall give you another Comforter [the Holy Spirit],
that he may abide with you for ever.

JOHN 14:16 KJV

Jehovah

I kneel before You at the church sanctuary altar, Lord God. No one else is here. Only the *whoosh* of warm air from the furnace breaks the silence. A sunbeam shimmers through the windows, casting its ray across the altar. It looks like a golden blessing, coming to me straight from heaven.

I adore You, Jehovah. How grateful I am, because You are my God. Your holy presence surrounds me. You fill me with a certainty of Your enduring love and care. You were in the beginning, You are now, and You shall be forevermore.

You are my Jehovah, my Yahweh. Many times You have whispered Your comforting words, *"I AM who I am. I will be who I will be."* Each time You do, I enjoy Your faithful, loving care.

You are above all else in heaven and earth. I love no other more than You, my God. When my health fails and my spirits sink, You still remain. When I become discouraged, You encourage and remind me that You are without end the great I AM. You are the strength of my heart. You are my God. Because You claim me as Your own, I know my inheritance with You forever is my heavenly prize.

I worship and adore You, my Jehovah, my Yahweh, my Everlasting God.

"Behold, God is my salvation,
I will trust and not be afraid;
'For YAH, the LORD,
is my strength and song.' "
ISAIAH 12:2 NKJV

King of Kings

*E*xalted are You, O King of all kings. I kneel in awe of Your holy name. When I consider Your glory, I tremble in Your presence. You alone are everlasting, surrounded by a pure, sweet light. There is no one as magnificent as You. You are Ruler and Creator of everything that exists. You place boundaries on the ocean edges. You declare their uninterrupted incoming and outgoing rhythm. Whenever they pitch and bellow, You are still in charge. Holy, holy, holy are You, O King of kings and Lord of lords.

You are my God, whom I worship and revere. I give thanks to You, my Lord, for Your love endures forever. You alone understand all things and do great wonders. You alone recognize the prayers of those who love and obey You.

You, my King of kings, can place people in honor and give them authority according to Your will. You care about world events, and they are in Your capable hands. You have power to appoint kings or presidents. You have power to remove them and set others in their stead when we call on Your name for help. You give wisdom to those who seek You and reveal truth to those who study Your Word.

How blessed You are, my Redeemer, King of kings, and Lord of lords.

*"He is Lord of lords and King of kings;
and those who are with Him are called,
chosen, and faithful."*

Revelation 17:14 NKJV

Scripture Index